South Shore Days 1940's & '50's

A collection of stories about growing up in the South Shore neighborhood of Chicago.

Gerald J. Lewis

South Shore Days 1940's & '50's

ISBN 978-0-578-02477-6

Printed in the United States of America.

Project Manager: Eric Lockstein
Professional Editing: Erin Augustine

Dedication

To the memory of Commander Phil Jordan, USCG. A good guy and a real family man, Peace Corps volunteer, Educator, OLP buddy, and South Shore historian par excellence. You were tempered in the forge of life and not found wanting. May we meet again.

Acknowledgements

I must give a great deal of credit to my son-in-law, Eric Lockstein, for his unswerving patience, advice, and support. Without him this project would never have been completed.

Caryn Lazar Amster, Bill Krueger, Pete Burns and my editor Erin Augustine also showed me the way and kept me on the path.

Msgr. Ignatius McDermott and the good Dominican Sisters from St. Catherine's in Kentucky are owed a great deal, as well as my classmates from the Our Lady of Peace Class of '52.

My family has been extremely and constantly supportive. I thank my wife, Peggy, and my daughters, Meg Lewis-Sidime and Pam Lockstein for their advice, support and patience in listening to these stories and more for so long.

Credit has to also be given to the Jewish community of old South Shore. Their unfailing intelligence and warm sense of humor helped us all to get along. Leo Kushner will always be remembered fondly by me.

Also, I owe a debt of gratitude to Reinhold Pabel, owner of the old "Book Mart' in Chicago Heights where I spent many hours while attending Bloom Community College in the early '60's.

Finally, an everlasting thanks to all of the "Chicago School" writers, Carl Sandburg, Upton Sinclair, Nelson Algren, Stuart Dybek, Ralph Ellison, Studs Terkel, David Mamet, Alan Ehrenhalt, James Baldwin and Saul Bellow. I will never be in their league but have enjoyed their talents, perseverance and contributions.

Preface

"I don't know anything that mars good literature
so completely as too much truth.
Facts contain a great deal of poetry, but you cannot use
too many of them without damaging your literature."

- Mark Twain

This is a memoir about growing up in Chicago in the 1940s and 1950s. The smaller setting is the old South Shore neighborhood nestled on Lake Michigan between Jackson Park to the north and the booming steel mills to the south.

While South Shore was a unique and special place, it was no better than many other neighborhoods of Chicago, or indeed any other big or small city. Chicago is a "city of neighborhoods," whether you are talking about Chinatown, Canaryville, Bridgeport, Beverly, South Chicago, Bronzeville, Hyde Park, Woodlawn or Englewood.

Any neighborhood in Chicago is essentially a small town. Visitors have difficulty believing this, but it is true. Each neighborhood has its own character and personality, depending on the culture and class of the people living there at any particular point in time.

My cousin, Dr. Bruce Hannon of the University of Illinois, used to say, “Good people make a good place good” when he would talk about his little hometown of Ivesdale on the prairies of central Illinois. South Shore was no different. Good people, some Irish or English or Russian or Scandinavian, Polish, Italian or German, made South Shore a very interesting place to grow up in the post-depression and war years. Catholics, Jews, Protestants and others got along well, most of the time.

We had block parties, victory gardens, and corn roasts. We had the Bluebirds, our own professional girls’ softball team, our own country club, our own IC railroad, our own lakefront, our own industrial area, parks, churches, shopping, libraries, taverns, restaurants, schools and theaters. In short, we were living in a very self-contained area. My family, and we were hardly alone, did not have our own automobile until I was sixteen. We walked or took a trolley or bus or taxi when we wanted to get around South Shore or downtown. Gasoline, oil and tires were either rationed or nonexistent. We did not have much money, but we never thought of ourselves as poor. Things were hard to get, but we never felt deprived. We just made do with what we had.

We were parochial, and Catholic and “parochial” had a dual meaning. One was the traditional religious one but the other was that of a very insular view of the world around us. It has taken us a lifetime of experience, education and living to learn that we were not the center of the universe and that there is a richness to be gained in learning about other people and their own rich cultures and different beliefs.

As rowdy and mischievous as we could be at times, we did OK in the long run. At least I don’t know that any of us went to jail or prison (overnights don't count).

As adults we became the American standard for the times: teachers, police officers and firemen, housewives, businessmen and women, priests and nuns and ministers. We became salespeople, lawyers, school administrators, writers, nurses, social workers, and airline pilots.

We are at a point of our lives now where we are looking back and trying to see the meaning in the times we went through and the meaning in our own lives. I find myself going back many times to those days of our youth in South Shore with great joy. I do not want to live in the past. The past is gone and we cannot bring back the old neighborhood as it was.

Please keep in mind that this memory trip is inherently true but memories are odd little things. They can change on you, slip away and become modified over time. Some of these stories are fact, some fiction and some fantasy. Some names have been changed to protect the innocent and some changed to protect the guilty. Overall the stories are true to growing up on Chicago's south side after the Great Depression and during WWII. It goes right up to 1952 when so many things started to change for all of us in Chicago and the country.

I know that we learned some basic values in those long ago days that we can still use today, no matter where life has taken us, or how big our families are or how our spiritual beliefs have changed. I feel we were fortunate to grow up where and when we did and I wish all good things to those families and children who have replaced us in South Shore. May you have as good a life and as rich a life as we have had.

Gerald J. Lewis on a Good Day

Contents

1

IRELAND FOREVER

A while ago I went out to Wyoming to visit my old Our Lady of Peace buddy Tom Murphy, and not surprisingly we went into Saratoga to look around. We had lunch at the old Wolfe Hotel and above the bar was this sign: "God invented whiskey so the Irish wouldn't rule the world."

You gotta love that, Irish or no, but like I always say, some stereotypes are true. Another stereotype is that the Irish are brawlers and fighters. You've no doubt heard of the Fighting Irish of Notre Dame. Here's one on that theme.

The story is about an Irish fighter from Pittsburgh, Billy Conn.

Billy was an up-and-coming light heavyweight in the 1940s weighing in around 180 pounds and with visions of a World Heavyweight championship. (Some called it "delusions of grandeur.") Trouble was, a guy named Joe Louis had the title at the time. That didn't bother Billy. He put on a couple of pounds, and coincidentally, Louis dropped weight and got down to 200. I suspect that was partly to increase his speed but also to show some of his inherent good sportsmanship. Louis was quoted at the time as saying, "He can run, but he can't hide."

Somehow the fight was arranged and took place in Madison Square Garden in June of 1941. It was a humdinger, with the cocky Conn taking the fight to Louis all through the early and middle rounds. Billy's manager told him in the last round that he was ahead on points and to get conservative and protect himself and he would coast to a victory by decision.

Conn was having nothing to do with that strategy. He said to himself, "I'm going to knock this bum out, if it's the last thing I ever do." Well, it almost was. Billy brashly opened up on the Brown Bomber, but made a critical mistake in leaving himself open, thinking that he had the fight made. Louis somehow pulled himself together and came up with a series of powerful counter-punches, followed by his classic lightning left jabs and finally the coup de gras: a blinding right hand that put Billy to sleep on the canvas.

Conn was carried back to his locker room semi-conscious, and when he was finally brought around, his manager asked him why he had disregarded his advice and blown the sure win. "Ah, what's the use," he said, one eye shut and grimacing in pain but with a wry smile, "of being Irish, if you can't do something stupid once in a while?" Oh, Billy boy, Billy boy, you were our charming Billy. In a way, Billy Conn summed up the whole Irish experience for many of our forbears and even us today.

The legacy lives on. The Irish are a complicated lot. By turns lovable, spiteful, charming, obnoxious, loyal, petty, steadfast, sly, brave, cowardly, trustworthy and untrustworthy, they are human to a fault with their heads in the clouds and then tripping on their feet. They might be knocking your head off one minute and buying you a drink the next, always both predictable and unpredictable, mercurial and yet introspective at the same time, singing and fighting altogether.

If you are Jewish or Polish or African-American or Italian or Hispanic or something else, and have ever run into the wrong side of the Irish, don't take it personally. They fight everybody and then, when there is nobody else, they fight each other. It's just doing business the Gaelic way. Here's the survival tip of the day for Chicago: if you are ever in a verbal joust about some beef or other, particularly with an Irishman, and he starts to call you "Pal," be careful. "Pal," among the South Side Irish, is not a term of endearment. It is a kind of cynical way of calling you an SOB and you'd best get ready for a sucker punch.

The Irish certainly have a love of language and learning, and if truth be told, saved Western civilization through their preserving the great books of antiquity in the Dark Ages and keeping a small flame of hope going when the world shut down for hundreds of years. Singing and fighting their way through history, struggling with tyranny, being religious and irreligious, reverent and irreverent, meeting life head-on and feet first. Generous to a fault, they can be as crafty as a gypsy if they need to be. In short, the Irish are survivors at heart and their innate sense of humor has stood them well through many vales and mountains. It still does.

Well, my mother's family was Irish. The Hannons. They were from around Newcastle in County Dublin, just west of Dublin City, where one piece of land is still called the Hannon bottomland. My mother's branch changed the spelling to Hannan somewhere down the line after they got to America. Supposedly this was done to avoid mixups in the mail between one Hannon clan or another living close by, but then why such a small change? If you really don't want your mail mixed up, change it to Grabowski, or Lefkowitz or Goldman.

Anyway, the Hannons held a "going away wake" for Andrew when he left the Newcastle area in the early 1840s and wound up in Hoosic Falls, New York. The family was reunited in Illinois when they moved there in the late 1840s. The old family story is they worked first on the Erie Canal and later the Illinois and Michigan Canal that ran from Bridgeport on the south side of Chicago to LaSalle on the Illinois River.

By the 1870s, Andrew's son Bernard was farming in Ivesdale in Champaign County. Bernard married, had a family, lost a wife, gained a wife, grew old and moved to Chicago. Things changed. By the 1920s his sons, my grandfather Joe and his brother Ed Hannan, had sold or rented out the farms in Central Illinois and moved to the South Shore neighborhood in Chicago where they built a two-flat at 7711 Constance Avenue, which they shared. Ed and Bridget, his stepmother, lived upstairs, and my grandparents Joe and Rowena lived on the first floor. Both Ed and Joe had backgrounds in electrical work, and family lore has it that great-uncle Ed designed the lighting for the Buckingham Fountain in Grant Park.

Joe Hannan worked for the Otis Elevator company for many years and put elevators in Chicago and all across the country. In the Roaring 1920s, he got into some scheme involving an automated parking garage in the Loop. This was a good blend of his electrical background and his elevator work. However, something happened with the partnership and the deal went south in the Depression. So it goes.

In 1967, my wife Peggy and I flew to England to find what we could about our families. We made the boat crossing to Ireland one rainy evening from Stranraer in Scotland to Larne in Northern Ireland. Although it was summer, the damp cold mist was numbing. We noticed small groups of passengers huddled under blankets on the top deck for an open air passage. It's hard to believe that earlier passengers from Ireland in the 1840s had made the much longer trip across the Atlantic, unprotected from the weather in the same manner, and under much worse weather conditions.

We were fortunate on our trip over to Ireland because we had a reserved cabin down below. Peggy tucked herself in for the night, but it was too early for me to turn in, so up to the saloon I went for a nightcap. I settled in to a comfortable lounge chair with my pint and began reading the paper. I soon noticed a group of young German tourists, obviously hikers complete with lederhosen, wool socks, boots and all, over in the far corner of the increasingly crowded lounge. They were having a jolly time, laughing and singing as if they were at the Oktoberfest in Munich.

Then I noticed a larger group of young Irish toughs, working men likely, with "Go-to-hell" caps and workboots on. They weren't singing but were casting some dirty looks over at the German kids. Something rang an alarm bell in my old Chicago defense system, and I began to look for the closest exit.

This went on for another five minutes, singing and muttering, when suddenly one of the construction crew stood up and threw his empty pint glass at the Germans, snarling, "Hey, ya fookin Krauts, shut your bloody traps! We don't need to listen to your sheet!" Crash! The glass shattered against the wall above the kids and all hell broke loose.

Since this was not my fight at all, I made a hasty but orderly exit down to our snug cabin. I had learned discretion was infinitely better than honor by this time in my life, but ten years before, at Aggie's Shamrock Inn on 67th Street, Chicago on St. Patty's night in 1957, I made the fateful decision to go help some dumb "Mick" in trouble, and that led to a whole host of things, none too good. It appeared I had at least learned something in a decade.

As I left the saloon to head down below, I turned and could see that all hell had indeed broken loose. It looked like a rugby scrum and a none-too-gentle one at that. From where I stood it looked like the German kids were getting the worst of the deal by far.

I got safely down to our cabin, and I think Peggy was surprised to see me return so soon. "A little disagreement upstairs," I said. "I thought I'd better come back down and live to survey the shambles in the morning."

True enough, early next morning I went up to see what I could see and the saloon indeed looked like a war zone. Much of the glass had been swept up and picked up, but windows were boarded up and taped, doors were sagging on their hinges, and furniture was piled up in two groups, broken and unbroken, or at least repairable.

We were now docked at Larne, and from what I could gather from the ship's crew, the local police had boarded the ship when it docked and taken the rowdies off to the local jail and the wounded to the local hospital.

On to Dublin we went. It surprised me that we were seeing so many junk yards and grimy, shabby areas. This was not the Glocca Morra I expected to find. On the trip from Belfast to the Republic, the train came to a lurching halt when we reached the border, and customs officers moved through the cars. We had not expected this and were a bit nervous, particularly since we had heard rumors of the "troubles" starting up again.

Our passports were checked and everyone was civil enough. Soon we were on our way into the capital city on the Liffey. Old Dublinh. Signs in Gaelic and English. A pub on every corner. Soon we saw the river and the Four Courts building, and we were in the heart of historic Dublin. We stayed at the Hotel Sherburne and with the weather brightening, decided to go out for a walk into the downtown area. As we were coming back, down O'Connell Street, we stopped at a traffic light. All of a sudden I heard a crack. I looked around in surprise, wondering. The light turned green and we were off with the evening rush hour crowds. When we were about half block away, Peggy turned to me and said, "Somebody hit me on the bottom back there with a rolled up newspaper." I did my best imitation of John Wayne in The Quiet Man but it was too late. It could have been anyone in the crowd and we agreed to consider it a complimentary but dumb Irish welcome to Dublin. I asked Peggy why she hadn't said anything when she got hit, and she said something about not wanting me to cause an international incident. Who, me?

We stayed in Dublin for a while, seeing all the local sights such as Kilmainham Jail, site of the executions of the Irish patriots in the 1916 Easter rebellion; Trinity College; out to Killarny and around to government offices to see if we could find any Hannons.

What we did not know and would not know until years later and had met my cousin Dr. Bruce Hannon from the University of Illinois, we were less than 20 miles from the Hannon Bottomland near Newcastle, just west of Dublin. Bruce and his son had hiked extensively in Ireland and have done much research on the Hannon clan, but we would have to wait for that chapter to open.

In my wanderings around Dublin that week, I had collected a ton of coins and was listing a bit with the weight in my pocket, not to mention the Guinness. I found myself exploring the pubs while Peggy was back at the Sherburne. It was rainy again, dark and misty with the light doing spooky things around the dark green, metal shamrock-bedecked light poles. (Maybe that was just one Black and Tan too many.) In any event, I found myself walking none too steadily over to the cheerfully lit pub on the next block and not paying much attention to anything when out of the misty shadows appeared a young raggedy woman carrying a soggy bundle in her arms.

"Please sir, a little sumthin' for me baby..." I did not think about it too much but didn't begrudge getting rid of the pecuniary weight, so I emptied my pockets of most of the heavy change. She expressed her thanks quietly and I was moving on when suddenly out of the same shadows I saw two of the biggest and toughest looking goons I had seen since my days in the old Workingman's Palace on West Madison Street's Skid Row. These characters were right out of Charles Dickens' and Bill Sykes' crew. They didn't say a thing but I was haunted by what might have happened if I had rejected her request, or worse, been obnoxious about it. I moved quickly into the next well-lit pub at the corner and eventually called a cab to the hotel. It was raining, you know.

That night we heard an explosion that was too close for our comfort. Soon we heard the sirens of the Gardas and the fire engines in the near distance. It turns out that the IRA had blown up a Dublin landmark, the Wellington column, erected by the British in a nearby square.

The "troubles" were starting again and a new generation of Orangemen would be on the move as well. We thought it best to bid adieu to the real Emerald Isle, the Holy Ground, and head to our summer course in London. We would march ourselves one day soon in the Chicago St. Patrick's Day Parade with the Plumbers from Local #130.

I can still hear my old buddy Murph singing his favorite ditty:

Oh the dirty, filthy Irish, they never wash their clothes;
That's because there's no Chinese laundries,

Where the River Shannon flows.

I can also still see Mike Royko's annual St. Patty's day column on the front page of the Chicago Daily News. The headline said simply, "Happy St. Patrick's Day to all the Irish on the Payroll." It was followed by a listing, column after column, of the names of all the Irish on the City of Chicago payroll. It was his biggest, and easiest, story of the year.

So, farewell to the Irish of Old South Shore, the Hannans, and the Shannons, the Melaniphys, McDonnells and McGraths, the Clarks, the McGreals and the Glynns, the Harkins and the Moriaritys , the Donovans, Sullivans and the Gerritys, the Mahers and the Figels, Grannans and the Sheehans. The Fagans and Coyles, Jordans and the Bouhans and the Buckleys, the Walls and the O'Briens, the Hugheses and the Judges, the Dunns and the Condons, the Fitzgibbons and the McCues, the Bohlings and the Sweeneys. The McNamaras and the Mcdermotts, the Delaneys the Coughlins and McCues and the McMahons.

Here's a toast to all the above and all the other South Side Irish not specifically mentioned:

OLD IRISH PRAYER

May those that love us, love us
And those that don't love us,
may God turn their black hearts,
And if He cannot turn their black hearts,
May He twist their ankles,
So we'll know them by their limping!

2

THERE WILL ALWAYS BE AN ENGLAND

Everybody has to be from someplace and the Lewises are no exception. The Lewis and Parker families were intertwined all the way back in England. They lived in a tiny place called Ketley Dingle, just outside the village of Ketley, near Wellington and not far from Shrewsbury in the county of Shropshire on the Welsh border. It's Wrekin country, the Wrekin being a distinct and unmistakable landmark hill in the middle of nowhere dropped there by a mythical giant who got tired of his heavy load.

The Midlands of England are an interesting mix of industry and magnificent scenery, with some of the most breathtaking long views in England alongside scenes from Hades: smoky iron foundries, mills, coke plants, and vile smelling factories right out of Victorian times, the sort that Charles Dickens would have recognized. Beautiful and lush Shropshire, looking for all the world like a Constable painting, was destined to become the birthplace of the Industrial Revolution, and the great iron bridge at Coalbrookdale was its icon.

Peggy and I flew to Britain the summer of 1967, a year after we were married, to look up our families: the Lewises and Parkers on my side, the Lynns and Deans on hers.

The Ketley area is a long way from Chicago and South Shore, but therein lies the tale. It reminded me very much of the great muscular industrial area on the southeast side of Chicago: Lake Calumet and the forest preserves juxtaposed with U.S. Steel, Bethlehem Steel, the everlasting coal yards, and the giant South Works, spewing flames and slag night and day in our youth.

How odd that we found letters in England from the emigrant Parkers to those still at home exhorting them to come to Chicago. "It is wonderful here," they exclaimed. They had found their own New World. "You don't have to take your hat off to any man and there are plenty of jobs after the big fire here," they wrote happily.

The letters must have paid off because soon the little Dingle with the three houses near the beautiful pond, Parker's Pool, was thinning out. There was the Darby house, connected to the old Quaker master builders of the Ironbridge foundries and old Abraham Darby himself and the two other houses. "Pool House" was home to the Parker family, and the third was the Lewis house itself.

In the thirty-plus years between our 1967 visit and our 2001 visit we have seen the old Lewis house transformed from a well-built habitation to an empty shell with weeds and vines growing through the open windows and castoff doors. In contrast, the old Parker home and farm were doing well on our last visit in 2001. The owner, elderly Mrs. Poole, who was living there alone and tending her gardens, invited us in, and I remember how proud she was of her remodeled kitchen and living room, which were done after her husband died.

On one side of the Dingle, if you discounted the power lines that ran toward Birmingham, was a gorgeous view of bright golden fields and rolling green hills, scattered lanes and hedgerows, and cattle grazing peacefully beyond Parker's Pool. It might be a 19th century painting, a place of serene, almost ethereal beauty.

On the other side of the pool, however, was the legacy of the Industrial Revolution: the great Sankey Iron Foundries with the encroaching black slag heaps getting higher, larger, and ever closer. It reminded me of How Green Was My Valley, both the book and the 1941 film.

"Over here," claimed the letters from Chicago, "When a man gets too old to work, they find him an easy job, a 'sitting down job' like counting nails!" (So much for Social Security.) The spiel went on: "and, you can go duck hunting on Lake Calumet after work."

The sales pitch must have worked: Alfred Lewis and his new bride, Alice Parker with her ten year old son, Albert, my grandfather, pulled up stakes and left their dear but doomed little Ketley Dingle for Chicago in 1892.

When Albert got on board the SS Lord Gough at Liverpool in April, he was Albert Parker. Shortly after they arrived in America, he had been transformed to Albert Lewis, no questions asked. A "shipboard adoption," they called it.

About eleven years before, young Alice Parker had been placed out as a servant girl in Manchester. Things happened. Alice found herself back in Ketley

Dingle as a single mother raising young Albert with the support of her family and friends, the village it takes to raise a child.

I can only imagine in that place and time it would have been an unforgiving situation. Ketley Dingle was small and even Ketley itself not a lot bigger. Social conditions and restrictions being what they were (you can read any of Thomas Hardy's novels for a peek) would have made life insufferable. Alfred Lewis' proposal came eleven years later, and the little family was off to a fresh start in the New World with her parents in Chicago.

I remembered my dad talking about Wellington, Ketley, and "the Dingle" so I knew where to begin searching in England. He was always proud of his English heritage, which he must have picked up from his father Albert and his grandparents. It has been suggested that Albert went back for a visit to Shropshire and Ketley in the early part of the 20th century, but of this there is no documentation.

I do know, however, that our family did not have any more contact with my English relatives until Peggy and I went over the summer after our marriage in 1966. How odd. All we had was our oral family history and a couple of place names, but there we were in at the Red Lion Inn in Wellington, the old market town between Shrewsbury and Ketley. So began the search.

We went to many of the local churches, like St. Mary's Redlake, and to more cemeteries than the local undertaker. We visited all the local libraries, government offices, city halls, justices of the peace, schools, funeral homes, genealogical societies, insurance companies, and banks, finding nothing. It was time to go. We were headed to London the next day. For some unknown reason, maybe fate, luck, intuition, or E.S.P., I decided to take one last stab at the mystery. I had seen a small pub in Ketley village called the White Lion on Watling Street, the old Roman Road to "Londinium." Peggy was done for the day, so off I drove alone (left hand side, thank you) into Ketley, trying to get there and back before dark. I went into the White Lion and found a place at the bar with the locals. After my first pint and upon ordering a second, the old barkeep said, "Well Yank, 'ow are you findin' things over 'ere?" I guess it didn't take the village idiot to figure out that I was not only not a local but was from America as well.

I told him a little bit about my family and that I was looking for the Lewises, Ben and Sam in particular were names I had from somewhere past, and that I was related to old Alfred Lewis and John Lewis, his younger brother. He grinned a toothless grin and cackled, "Ah, ye've coom' to just the right place, Yank. Yer relations are just oop the hill behind 'ere! Joan Jones she is now, but she was a Lewis through and through." He hooted down to the end of the bar to a stocky, middle-aged chap. "Say Charlie, be a good 'un and run this Yank up to Joan's house." Turning back to me, he explained that Joan and her husband Don Jones did not have a phone.

So Charlie and I quickly finished our pints and shoved off, none too steadily, in his dilapidated old heap. When we sputtered to the top of the hill we came to series of council flats. Charlie pulled over, beeped the horn, and hollered into the open door, "Oh Joan, hey Don, your Uncle Alf's boy from Chicago is here to see you!" Joan appeared first. She was a small, neat and tidy lady in an apron, just finishing the supper dishes.

If she was surprised she didn't show it. She got right down to business. "My goodness gracious," she said quietly, shaking her head. "After all these years... Come in, come in. You are really home now." I was, too.

Don Jones came out to see what all the fuss was about, and we got old Charlie on his way back down the hill with a tip for another pint and set about putting all the pieces of the puzzle together after a half century of separation.

Joan Lewis Jones, it turns out, was John Lewis's daughter and old John was Alfred Lewis' younger brother, still living at 92. We would meet him shortly, but for now we had some talking to do and even more looking at old pictures of my new family. I really felt that I was home again.

I think that one of the highlights was going out to the local pub with Don, Joan, and old John Lewis. As we went to cross the street, Peggy reached out to take John's arm. He was having none of that, thank you very much, and shook her off with a swat. When the drinks showed up in the ancient but comfy pub, I went to pay, but it was my turn to get the swat. There was a sharp crack on the back of "me hand" and a reprimand to follow. He was a Lewis all right.

We cancelled our trip to London and decided to stay a while in the Wellington and Ketley area.

We visited John's nephews, Ben and Sam Lewis. Both men were in their seventies but still active and engaged in heavy physical labor, loading lorries with tons of brick by hand each working day. They were as strong and robust as could be. My hope was that some of those genes had made their way to me.

We met cousins by the dozens, visited local graveyards with Joan and Don, and, in short, got caught up after generations of separation. They were puzzled, in a way, with our interest in all of this. They had been surrounded by the past all their lives and could hardly comprehend the curiosity we felt about our place of origin. After a week or so, we headed for London, as we were scheduled for a two-week summer course on Education in Britain and then home.

I will always treasure a small plaid notebook that Joan Jones gave me in Wellington on our 2001 trip. In her clear and precise handwriting, she had listed the names, relationships, telephone numbers and tidbits of historical interest of family members. It was the perfect gift, and I resolved to try to keep the circle unbroken and to try to get the next generation interested in their rich British heritage. So far, not much luck. However, we live in hope.

Through family stories and my research, I've learned that the Alfred Lewis family arrived on the "Lord Gough" at Philadelphia on May 9, 1892. I don't know how or when they got to Chicago, but I assume that they left directly by train and were met by the Parkers in the Windy City, which was feverishly preparing for the 1893 Columbian Exposition.

Alfred, Alice and young Albert quickly settled into the Englewood neighborhood with relatives and later moved to 5652 S. Atlantic Ave. which today is Wells Avenue. You can see the house as you zip down the Dan Ryan expressway (unless there's construction). All the homes on the east side of Wells were torn down for the roadway, but luckily the old house still stands on the other side.

Alfred went to work for the Rock Island railroad, whose tracks are just east of the expressway. He was severely injured in a railroad accident and died as a result of that in August 1925. Two other children had been born to the new family in Chicago, Joseph W. and Edwin. My grandfather Albert went to work early, as kids did in those days, eventually getting on with Union Carbide as an office boy downtown in the Loop, and in true Horatio Alger fashion, rose to be a vice president.

Albert married Ethel Dearborn Long in October 1906 in Chicago, and they had three children: Albert in 1908, Dorothy in 1909 and my dad, Donald, in 1911. Ethel died of tuberculosis in the summer of 1913. She is the grandmother I never knew, a 27-year old girl forever. Her monument says eloquently, "My Girlie."

Albert then placed Albert Junior and Donald in Lawrence Hall, an Episcopal orphanage on the Northwest side of Chicago where they lived until the 1920s. My Aunt Dorothy, who may have initially gone to Alfred and Alice's home on Wells Street, later attended school in Iowa and then worked for a wealthy family in Lake Forest. My Grandfather Lewis got on with his career, getting an apartment in South Shore, first on East 77th and then in the mid-1930s at 7735 S. Constance, just down the street from the Hannans at 7711. Albert finally remarried in the 1940s and lived a few blocks north of us at 72nd and Clyde by St. Phillip Neri.

All three of the grandparents I knew died within a few months of each other in 1960. My Grandfather Lewis passed away in April in Lakeland, Florida, and both the Hannans at their country home in Cedar Lake, Indiana; Joe in July and Rowena in September. My younger brother Donnie died at age 18 in June of that fatal year.

The immigration chapter was over. We were here to stay and new generations would follow, beginning new chapters with their families.

3

GOD BLESS FATHER 'MAC'!

God bless Father Ignatius McDermott.

I have never met another like him and probably never will. Anyone whose life he touched has never forgotten him. He was a great combination of so many traits and all of them good. He was pious but not sanctimonious. He was 'otherworldly' and yet down-to-earth. Generous to a fault, he also possessed an innate sense of frugality and humility. He was patient and kind, yet was said to have a blowtorch temper.

He was a man's man and enjoyed his sports, yet could be as easy as the old Ace comb guy: "Tough but gentle." Father Mac came to Our Lady of Peace as an associate pastor to Father (later Monsignior) Henry Friel in 1941. He stayed until 1946 when something changed his entire mission.

He was officially working with the Archdiocese of Chicago downtown somewhere, but unofficially he began to work with all the derelicts of life who were in a down and out limbo until Father Mac went to Skid Row. He started with nothing and parlayed that into a thriving 35 million dollar non-profit organization dedicated only to the welfare of the homeless, the friendless, and addicts of all kinds. Haymarket House on Washington

Boulevard continues working with drug addicts and alcoholics.

Always the Irish rebel, he used charm, wit and grace to build an empire for good. Yet he never lost touch with his common roots, no matter how many awards he won or banquets he attended in his honor. He could have been mayor of Chicago if he had wanted to be.

I wondered sometimes what it would have been like if he had just settled down in South Shore with a Colleen, Kathleen, or Eileen and raised twelve little McDermotts in a big white house at 80th and Constance. I am sure that life would have been wonderful for that family, but things would been different for Bedford Falls.

Father Mac was one in a million. A million priests that is, not people. I feel blessed to have known him as well and for as long as I did. I still have his last Christmas card. I haven't opened it yet. I will someday. God bless Father Mac.
God bless us, too.

A DIAMOND JUBILEE FOR FATHER MAC

April 21, 1996
Haymarket House
Chicago, Illinois

9:00 a.m. Be There, or be Square, but Be On Time!

"Introibo ad Altare Dei.
Juventutem Meam"
"Hold <u>everything</u>—we got some straight talking to do..."
Ruddy faced, snowhaired, warm focused old priest:

SOUTH SHORE DAYS – 1940's & '50's

Gentle-voiced but always straight talking:

"I have a concern" he says quietly,
looking us in the collective eye.
There's too much talking around here, I fear,
We have a problem; I have a problem; you have a prob-
lem!
Seems there's too much talking altogether.
'Specially during communion.
(Turns out: Father "don't 'low that 'round here.")

"You've got 48 'days' a week to do your own thing,
least you can do is give God a few hours on Sunday."
(Pardon me, Father. <u>You've</u> got 48 days a week to give.
No Freudian slip here either.

This man puts in that kind of time.
After hours come more visits.
You name it: hospitals, lockups, flophouses and more.
The alkies, the halt, the profane, and the druggies.)
That familiar South Side 'Visitation-Irish' accent
continues: (we're not off the hook yet).
"If you want to talk to each other during mass,
go outside," he said.
"Take a hike around the block and
have a filibuster with yourself!"
This is oldline, flatout authority talking here.
No wishy-washy-whiney stuff.
You want choices?
You got 'em:
"Keep quiet during my mass
or take a hike!"
Father Friel's ghost has got to be smiling.
We poke each other in the ribs;
PJ tells me he's having a flashback.

GOD BLESS FATHER 'MAC'!

We are home again.
Father Mac, we love ya.

The mass is begun.
Let's Play Ball!

LOCAL BASEBALL SCORES:

SECOND INNING
Bethlehem shelled by Jerusalem 12-zip;
Nazareth edges Nablus 5-4.
The mass goes well, but it is not the "Altar of <u>our</u> Youth."
It is facing the wrong way for one thing.
Father Mac's mistress is pain. You can see it in every move.
He had a shot at the old football Cards
when they were at 61st and Normal.
Now the leg gives him no relief.
Pain management they call it.
He calls it work.
God's work.
Our work.

THIRD INNING
(Gaza rips Hebron 14-2; Jericho squeaks
By Beersheba 1-zero!)

The Gospel according to St. Luke:
"On the Road to Emmaus."
Everyone stands; we have no books but we follow PJ and
then sit for the Homily.

FOURTH INNING
(Tyre 6, Sidon 2; Emmaus 8, Samaria 4.)
Father Mac talks about the puzzled disciples getting
"knocked out of the box."
Sports analogies abound.
(Last weekend it was Pilate 3, good guys zip.
Now, the score is almost even:
Dismas is in Paradise
and Jesus has 40 days of spring training
before taking the show on the road.)

FIFTH INNING
(Tiberias vs. Cana [called because of rain. Rain?])
The Homily continues.
The twenty-seven Black Madonnas are restless.
Crack cocaine moms
In Sunday best, they look oddly enough like old OLP-
ers:

Navy blue jumpers, light blue blouses and white sox,
You knew it would be White Sox!
Father Mac must've picked them out.
Father Mac, we love ya!

SIXTH INNING
Father Mac is just getting warmed up.
Like an old Sox knuckleballer past his prime,
He leads off with an apology of sorts:
"I don't mean to be the
'President of the Pessimist Corporation of America'"
"I try to be an optimist... "
Then comes the litany of "The Lost City"
like déjà vu all over again:
mad bombers, children killing their parents;

parents killing their children;
kids throwing kids off balconies at the Projects.
He reminds us of the loss of civility.
"Thank you; Please; Pardon me; You're welcome!
Where has it all gone-and why?"
We are surprised to hear what we took for granted.
Even the Big Corporations are not
spared Father Mac's "Dies Irae"
"Where is loyalty," he asks. "Where are the old values?"
"What happened to their Game Plan?"

SEVENTH INNING
The Offering:
"This is not a wafer!" he growls.
(No transubstantiational-philosophical debate needed
here.)
He's made a believer out of me.
"This is the true body and the true blood of
Our Lord and Savior, Jesus Christ!"
I don't hear anybody talking.
The only filibuster is on the altar.

EIGHTH INNING
We have communion together for the
first time since 1952.
Where has the time gone?
How about a game of Ledgeball after mass?
Get the Sunday Trib from Old Addie and stop in at Mo's
to get a Mrs. Hackel's sweet roll and a Pepsi.
Haven't eaten since midnight.
(Carmel vs. Leo at Eckersall - are you going?)

NINTH INNING
It's cleanup time.
Ite, Missa est!

The crowd disappears.
We don't go, we've got a gift to give.
Some say that Father Mac's a saint.
I don't know about that!
But I do know,
He's one 'hellava' man!

EXTRA INNINGS
I find Father in the sacristy, people buzzing around;
Most have come in from the tonier suburbs—old friends.
Father Mac looks beat.
Slumped on a sofa resting for the next round.
"Come in," he says,
"Gerry, PJ, Boys, I'm glad to see ya!"
We file in and get comfortable.
The stories are about to begin.
Our Mick is in fine fettle; wasn't he a quiet kid once?
Jimmy Enright, David "In the Wake of the News" Condon
John "The Barber Shop" Carmichael.
All good South Shore people.
All alive again.
Blind baseball players,
Father Friel, Father Tom Bryne, Fathers Tom and Bill Maher, Father Figel:
Our own Sister Jean Joseph, a.k.a. Pat Hughes
all get an honorable mention.
Get this:
Father Mac remembers giving the
Tilden Tech team a blessing
before the Kelly Bowl
In Soldier Field, 1940 - something.
Thirty of thirty-three of Coach Chuck Harvey's
kids are Catholic.
(It's like an inter-squad game!)

GOD BLESS FATHER 'MAC'!

Was it against Weber or Fenwick?
Doesn't matter, you can look it up. The main thing is the
Tilden kids had felt abandoned by their church,
Fact is,
No kid is abandoned when Father Mac is around.
He told us about the "big guys" at OLP
getting in trouble over fireworks.
Wound up in Grand Crossing station courtesy of car 147.
Father Mac talked to the Commander:
"I want these kids out of here now;
before I tell everybody what your real name is."
(The kids were back at OLP in less than a half hour.)
Father Mac, we love ya!
He twists and mangles the gift card, rolls it up, maybe
Kay'll press it out. Tomorrow.
Opens the blue and green wrapped box:
An autographed,
a framed picture of Luke Appling.
"Old Aches and Pains" himself—#4. Hall of Fame. Listen.
"Those aren't boos," my dad said to me.
"The crowd's calling his name."
"C'mon LUUUKE, c'mon LUUUUUUKE!"
Craack! Foul ball. The crowd loves it. It's his signature:
3, 7, 9, 11 foul balls on a good day—the pitcher is ticked.
Wearing down.
Then:
Craaaack: a line drive single over second.
THE CROWD IS ON ITS COLLECTIVE FEET!
Luke threatens to take second but brakes,
laughing, skids back to first.
The original "Cool Hand Luke" has done it again.

We leave the sacristy as Father heads
off to other friends waiting.
Off to the Wishbone for a brunch.
Father Mac, we love ya!
We are standing talking outside the "Big" Chapel
when the door opens with a bang!
Pat Barth does a Wily Coyote imitation:
flattened against the wall. We meet Jim McHugh.
Jim is all apologies for being late
but graciously offers us a tour.
Father Mac's right-hand man from the old neighbor-
hood:
Visitation parish at 55th and Halsted –
a special place for the South Side Irish.
Father Mac's old neighborhood, and James Farrell's.
Jim McHugh is at Haymarket every day –
seven days a week.
A chip off the old block,
He is devoted to Father Mac, you can tell.
We go upstairs.
In the Day Room,
we find the twenty-seven Black Madonnas.
Shoes off, white sox gleaming.
Relaxing, talking, smiling.
Watching T.V.
A black preacher evangelizing with a 1-800 number.
(Get your credit card ready!)
(Father Mac did not even take up a collection.)
Mick outdoes the black preacher.
(What happened to that quiet little kid we knew?)

"Hello ladies, everybody having a great day?
Yes, we are all having a great day!
Smiles and white teeth all round.

GOD BLESS FATHER 'MAC'!

Ite, Ballgame est.

We love ya, Father Mac!

4

FIRST CONFESSION AND "THE LOSS OF INNOCENCE"

I can remember it like it was yesterday. It was May again. The springtime of 1946. We were getting ready to make our First Communion.

FIRST CONFESSION AND
"THE LOSS OF INNOCENCE"

Our Lady of Peace church at 79th and Jeffery Boulevard on the southeast side of Chicago was really two churches. The first one was in the basement downstairs and was like a bomb shelter, with huge columns holding up a low ceiling.

This was the original OLP, constructed after WWI in 1919 by Father Rice after he returned from France. For the next twenty-odd years when times were good, they worked on the "big church." This was the upstairs edifice with its Romanesque architecture that included the landmark Italianate bell-less tower that could be seen for blocks around.

The lower church was for kids. Mass every Sunday and Holy days downstairs. We were not allowed to go to mass upstairs with the grownups until we were at least in high school.

There were a few exceptions. It was the spring of second grade, and ours was the one exception. The magnificent upper church was awash in perfume. Flowers were everywhere in honor of our Blessed Mother. Springtime was especially welcome on the south side of Chicago after a long winter. The area became totally bleak and grimy from the thousands of coal fires around the neighborhood as well as the windborne soot from the steel mills over on the lake and dirty old newspapers danced with the winds back and forth across 79th Street in front of the church with every passing trolley.

We were seven years old now, the so called, "age of reason" when you were supposed to know right from wrong and act accordingly. Later on, we ran into some people who didn't seem to get to the age of reason until much, much later, if at all.

This, however, was a landmark occasion in our growing up—a real milestone for us with confirmation, graduation, and high school all in the distant future. Our grade school was divided into two sections named for the streets nearest to that side. The Chappel side was on the east side of the building with the Jeffery side on the west. The two sets of classes rarely worked together, or interacted in any way. If you lived east of the church and school, you went to the Chappel side and if you lived west of Jeffery all the way to Stony Island Avenue you went to the Jeffery side. There were some exceptions, but not a lot, and I think all the dispensations had to go to the Pope in Rome, which is why there weren't too many and why they took so long to return.

We had a wonderful nun that year on the Chappel side. Her name was Sister Margaret Ann and she was a beautiful person, very young as many of the sisters were and with a nurturing personality that we all needed and appreciated. Most of our nuns came from rural backgrounds and she probably was no different.

Our nuns were Dominicans from St. Catherine's Mother House near Bardstown in Kentucky. They did not, as a rule, have a great deal of education, but they had at least a two-year certificate for teaching. They were overloaded with crowded classes, a bunch of rough and tumble kids, and low pay, if anything, as our tuition was only a dollar a month. They led a regulated life without many of the freedoms that we take for granted. They were certainly junior saints, if not full-fledged ones yet.

I don't know when we began practicing for our first communion but it would probably have been after Christmas vacation.

"Who made you?"
"God made me."
"Why did God make you?"
"God made me to know Him, to love Him and to serve

Him in this world and to be happy with Him in the next."

It went on, and on and on. We drilled and reviewed and practiced walking in straight solemn lines without any horseplay or nonsense, especially when we were practicing upstairs in the big church with the kids from the Jeffery side.

The moment of truth was fast approaching and we were getting more anxious by the day. What if we made a mistake up at the altar? What if we tripped and fell down in front of the whole congregation like my grandfather Joe Hannan, who was then literally kicked off the altar at St. Joseph's church in tiny Ivesdale, Illinois, never to enter a Catholic church again until his death in 1960 when he couldn't say, "no, thank you" anymore.

I remember him sitting out in front of OLP church in his huge 1936 Oldsmobile reading the Sunday Chicago Tribune, funnies and all, waiting for my grandmother to get out of mass.

Even more unnerving to us was the thought of making our first confession. What were we going to say? What sins had we really committed? We had to say something. Could we make stuff up? Wasn't that then just another sin? We were worried. Some of us were beyond worry. We were petrified. Frozen. Done for. What were we supposed to say? What were we going to do?

I thought of my buddy Tom Murphy. Murph would have the answer. I left our basement apartment at 7952 Phillips, cut through the prairie (a vacant lot to you) and crossed the alley to Murph's place on Yates. Murph was better off than we were, as his folks owned a three-flat building on Yates Boulevard. "Free and clear," as they say, "In like Flynn!" His family had two Jewish families paying the rent on time and Murph had a built-in side job of turning on the lights and lighting the stoves for the Friday Sabbath next door at Congregation Agudath Achim.

I didn't want to climb three floors if I didn't have too, so the deal was to let loose with a loud hoot: "EE-YOoo Murpheeee!" A couple of these and Murph would appear if he wasn't already sentenced to hard labor. His dad had been severely burned in an accident in the nearby steel mills and always reminded me afterwards of James Cagney in White Heat, swathed like a mummy with his third degree burns. Murph really learned about hard work taking care of his dad and that three-flat as a kid.

In fact, at age seven, Murph had to get home right after school every day to give his dad a morphine shot or two until his Ma got home from her job as a ticket seller for the IC commuter line. The net result was that Murph had to do all the janitorial jobs around the building and he grew up in a hurry.

We were always in the same class at OLP and now getting ready for the same big event. We sat on his third floor back porch, looking out over the railroad tracks, our prairie, and the rows of apartment buildings and tried to figure out what to do about our first confession.

"Murph, what are we supposed to say? What did we ever do that was so bad?"

"I don't know." He looked worried. "Maybe we'll just have to make up some stuff."

"Like what?" I asked. "We really haven't had too much time to do too many bad things."

"Hey," he said brightly. "How about that time you shot me in the arm with an arrow?"

"Aaw, c'mon Murph! That was an accident and you know it. Besides, my old man came right away and pulled the arrow out, bandaged you up and gave you a buck! You got nothin' to complain about and that was not no sin nohow!"

"Well," he said, "how about the time I got that axe for my birthday and you took it and chopped down that tree on the telephone wires, and the MPs came in jeeps and took my axe away and called our folks?"

"Hey Murph, c'mon. You know that was an accident too. It wasn't like we were trying to wreck the phones. It just happened. We aren't lumberjacks you know."

"Well, what about the time we let the air out of all the tires of the cars up at Eckersall Stadium when Mount Carmel was playing Leo?"

" Oh Murph, you really got a good memory for some things and then in school it's like you can't remember nothin'. You're really not much help at all."

"I'm just tryin' to help," he protested. "What about the time you dug that foxhole in the prairie path and old man Goldstein fell in it?"

"MURPH...You know as well as I do that was an accident too. How could we know that he would be coming that way on that night? Besides, we said the right prayer for him."

"What's that?" Murph asked.

"Remember? In the name of the Father, and the Son and...into the 'Hole He Goes!'" We both laughed at that one.

"Well, Murph said thoughtfully, " yeah, but we didn't have to cover the hole over with sticks and cardboard and leaves and dirt. Besides, it was your idea to put all that broken glass in the hole."

"Well, yeah, that was kinda bad, I guess. I thought the Essex gang would come that way tryin' to wreck our fort, but he shouldn'a been drinkin' so much or he would've seen it instead of falling in like a jerk. So really, it was his fault as much as ours." Silence.

"Hey Murph," I asked, "you live next to a synagogue, right?"

"Well, so what, I get paid every week to go over on their Sabbath to turn the lights off and on and light the stoves and the boiler in the winter."

"You got a good deal, that's for sure, but do the Jewish kids have to go to confession like us?"

"Well," Murph said frowning, "I don't know but I don't think so from all I've seen over there. Hey, but they do have a really good deal when they get a little older. They get to go to some bar and they get all kinds of presents and money. I think it kind of makes up for Christmas!"

"What? They never have to go to confession and they get a deal like that?" I asked in amazement. "That just goes to show you that life just ain't fair. Maybe we should be Jews."

Murph threw up his arms in mock horror. "Not me, buddy, never and no how!"

"I didn't think you were all that religious, Murph."

"Maybe I am and maybe not, but I know they would cut off the end of my weiner and that is just not gonna happen," he said, shaking his head. I could see it was really upsetting him so I decided not to push the issue. It scared me too.

We were getting nowhere fast now so we decided to split up and talk about it on the way home after school tomorrow. We didn't have much time though as our

First Communion was in two weeks and our First Confession even sooner.

The marching, drilling and memorizing went on incessantly. Time was running out on us. The boys were getting fitted for new white suits and our first pair of real pants. No more knickers! The girls, meanwhile, were getting their new white dresses and veils.

Now we had more worries. Our beloved Father McDermott, or Father Mac,, was rumored to be moving to the Archdiocese downtown and leaving the parish.

We were heartbroken but even more scared that we would have to go to confess our sins, such as they were, to Father Jordan, otherwise known as "No Nonsense" Jordan. He was everything that Father Mac was not. Father Mac was warm, kind and friendly. He always had a laugh for you or a pat on the head or a light punch in the stomach if he knew you could take it.

The real kicker was this: what if Monsignor Friel was in that box? Now that was frightening! Old Man Friel ruled the parish with an iron hand. Rumor had it that he was a real skinflint when it came to giving anything to anyone especially the good sisters who were working for a pittance anyway. Irish born and stern looking, without a shred of humor, he looked like he had been raised on blighted potatoes and vinegar and had a disposition to match. He was a real sourpuss but lived like a king in one of the best parishes in Chicago while many of the parishioners were struggling to make ends meet.

There it was. The confessional itself. A grim box shrouded in mystery whose walls had seen and heard it all. It had three doors, really: a large center area for the Father-confessor and two smaller doors for the penitents on either side with sliding screened windows. One of the spookiest things was the eerie red light over each of the doors for the penitents. The light went on when the penitent knelt down to begin their confession.

It was now the Friday before First Communion Sunday and we were finally up in the big church upstairs and getting ready to make our first confession. Boys were on one side of the church, and girls on the other. We eyed each other warily. What could the girls be going to confess? What had they ever done wrong? I sure would like to know that.

The boys looked like they wanted to be out in the school yard on this glorious May day. We could be playing ledge ball or "slaughteration," which was a giant game of keep-away involving the boys from two or more classes in a no holds barred kind of early Rugby game. We could be doing anything rather than to be here, inside the upper church with all the eyes of the statues and saints of long ago watching us and waiting.

All the "brains" and scholars seemed to go first. The regulars all dawdled, shifted around and mumbled their way along as they tried their best to somehow disappear. The first two boys out were Jim Sherman and Terry Tobin, always high favorites with the nuns. They seemed to be smiling a little bit as slid back to their pews and adjusted their halos.

"Mac is back," they whispered. "Father Mac is here!" Glory be and hallelujah, Father Mac is back with us again. It seemed like a miracle. We were going to be saved!

The red light in front of me went out. The penitent slithered out, eyes downcast. I was done for. There was no going back: the old die was cast and the Rubicon was crossed. This was it.

I was in the booth and could hear this great priest finishing up with whoever was on the opposite side. "Go and sin no more..." came across faintly. Well, that didn't seem too bad. Maybe there was hope after all.

My screen cover slid open with a small bang. I jumped, and then sped into my two second rehearsed spiel: "Bless-me-father-for-I-have-sinned-this-is-my-first- confession-I-was-disobedient-to-my-parents-ten-times-I-was-late-to-school-twiceI-pushed-my-brother-once-I, I, I..."

"Son, son, take it easy, slow down and think about what you are saying," came the gentle voice of our old Father Mac with that hint of an Irish brogue mixed in with his Chicago accent. "You don't have to rush things and you don't have to make things up" the voice said in a steady, calm and reassuring way. "You need to really examine your conscience and confess to God those things that are really bothering you. Particularly those things that you might have done to hurt someone else."

"Yes, Father, but, but I really don't have much to confess at all."

"Then, my son, you are lucky indeed. Just remember that this is a trial run for you and your classmates right now. This is a time to learn how to think about the things that you have done and about those things that you have not done but you should have done. Do you see that?"

I wasn't quite sure about that but said slowly, "Yeesss, Father."

"Good boy. Then for your penance I just want you to fix one thing that you have done that you shouldn't have done. Make it up to whoever you may have hurt in some way, no matter how small. Can you do that?" Silence. "Yesss, Father, I can try..."

"In addition then," he whispered, "I want you to say one 'Our Father,' one 'Hail Mary' and one 'Glory Be.' Can you do that?"

"Yes, Father, I think I can." I said meekly.

"Then," he said, (and I heard him smile) "go and sin no more."

"Thank you, Father." I walked out of that confessional like walking on air. I had made it. I survived and lived to tell about it. I could handle anything now. First Communion would be a piece of cake.

That next Sunday dawned bright and beautiful. It was sunny with the temperature in the low seventies. I got my white suit ready to go and got some help from Dad with my tie. It was a white hand-knitted beauty done by my grandmother. I must have looked like an angel.

Off we went, walking as a family down 79th Street. We didn't have a car then. Not many people did then, just after the war. It would be another five years or more before production got back into full swing.

Everything went well at the mass. No one misbehaved or fell down or threw up. In short, all the kids were stellar. Beautifully dressed and on their best behavior.

What a great day. Father Mac was up on the altar with the two grumps but we didn't care about them as long as he was there with us. There was a kind of tea after mass with our favorite, Mrs. Hackel's bakery goods. We were in pig heaven, so to speak, and did our best to keep our beautiful white suits and dresses immaculate.

We were home before noon and most families had company coming over to celebrate the occasion. We were no exception and grandparents, aunts, uncles, cousins and neighbors all came over with gifts and cards.

Murph and I were allowed to take some of our gift money and go up to the White Castle at 79th and Essex, white suits, ties and all, and get some nickel sliders for a special lunch. I think we had a whole dollar and we spent it all on a bag of the greasy delights, smothered in onions, with pickles on top.

We fully intended to walk all the way back to my house and eat them there but it was just too nice a spring day, sunny and warm with a gentle breeze coming down 79th Street from the lake.

"Hey Murph," I said, "let's have just one apiece, man. I'm starvin'."

"I don't know" said the guardian of the bag. "Nobody can eat just one of these babies!"

"Well then, make it two, dammit."

Murph feigned shock. "Ooh, what did you say, and on our First Communion day, too."

That did it. I didn't have much patience to begin with and that broke the old camel's back. I grabbed the bag but he was holding on like an Irishman to his whiskey. We started scuffling back and forth, pulling on the bag in a tug o' war, slipping and sliding on the new black cinders in the now crowded parking lot. A car just missed us, and when the driver screamed at us we gave him the bird and laughed. He slammed on the brakes and the hot rod fishtailed to a stop, narrowly missing another car. "You dumb asses, I'm gonna kick your butts," he yelled. Then he thought better of it and floored the car, sending up a spray of black cinders as he roared out of the lot.

Just then the bag split in two, dumping the sliders in their little cardboard castle boxes all over the cinder lot. That was it for what little patience I had left. "Look at what you did now," I yelled. "You stupid squat!" Other cars in the parking lot were really getting into it now: guys laying on their horns and egging us on, girls laughing and singing, car radios blaring. We were at it tooth and nail. We were rolling on the ground in the cinders as black as the volcanic ash on Iwo Jima. We grabbed at each other, kicked, smashed, scratched, cussed, and cried.

We rolled over the burgers, mashing them into the ground and not caring any more about anything except to annihilate each other. It was not a pleasant sight, except to all the older teens who thought it a hoot. They were all laughing and hollering to beat the band. Our formerly white suits were ruined now and my handmade tie was in shreds. We looked like we had been shoveling coal in the steel mills for a week. We were both bleeding and I had a black eye.

We began to pick up the ruined burgers and throw them at the cars in the lot. Very quickly other cars started in on the food fight and soon the whole lot was throwing burgers, fries, shakes and cokes at each other and us.

We decided to take off and head home as quick as we could. The older guys were in hot pursuit but we had an advantage. We knew the alleys and the shortcuts through the prairies behind the White Castle and we headed for our underground fort like a couple of prairie dogs being pursued by foxes. We dove in headfirst. We were safe for now!

We waited down in the cool of the dugout, trying to catch our wind and wishing that we had a couple of ice cold Cokes. It was hot and we were miserable. What more could go wrong?

From where we were dug in, we could just see my side yard on Phillips. There were our folks, their friends and neighbors, brothers and sisters and cousins by the dozens. Everyone eating, laughing, playing and talking. We felt like dropping into a hole. Then we remembered. We were in a hole already. We wished we had our shovels. Maybe we could make it even deeper.

We looked out again and there it was: the Monsignormobile. The Monsigiormobile was a big, long and shiny black Caddy with fins. We were dead! Monsignor Friel was paying a rare visit around the neighborhood. The only good thing was that Father Mac was with him and Father Jordan too. Nick the maintenance man was the chauffeur. What more could go wrong, just went wrong!

Murph and I looked at each other. We were tired, hungry, dirty and bloody. The ghost was up. It was time to go and face the inevitable. We crawled out of our bunker and headed across the prairie towards my yard and the party.

"Ma, Ma, there they are," screamed my little brother helpfully. We weren't going to sneak in unnoticed. The grownups ran to get to us, everybody talking at the same time.

FIRST CONFESSION AND "THE LOSS OF INNOCENCE"

"Are you OK? "What happened to you?" "Where have you been?" Everybody was talking at once.

"Jesus, Mary and Joseph," my dad said. Then: "Sorry about that, Fathers! No offense meant! So, what happened to you boys, I want to know NOW!"

I began to shake a bit, close to tears and Murph was not far behind. "We got jumped by the big guys from the Essex Gang up at White Castle," I answered, looking down a bit and away. "They beat us up and took our hamburgers. We tried to stop them, but they wouldn't listen."

"OK then" my dad said, "We'll just get you guys cleaned up and then we'll go back up there and look for them and you can pick them out. Go on now, wash up and get your play clothes on."

"Dad," I said pleadingly, "they took off by now. They were on their bikes and headed towards the lake when we left."

"Well, we'll see about that," he gruffed in his low, serious voice. "We'll just see about that!"

The priests were quiet. Nick the driver was stuffing himself with my grandmothers tollhouse cookies—my favorite! They were disappearing fast.

Father Mac came over and put his big arms around us. "You guys are all right now," he said quietly. "You're safe and no one is going to hurt you." He went with us to our basement apartment.

After a couple of minutes of silence I blurted out "Father, it didn't really happen that way. We just got in fight and then dropped our lunch and, and..."

"Then things just kind of got unraveled, didn't they?" he said kindly. "That's what happens when you don't tell the truth right away. Things just unravel and you have to keep lying to catch up. You meant well but things just got worse, didn't they?"

"Yes, Father," we both said in unison. "It just got worse."

Then he told us that he had to go but he would pray for us that we would do the right thing now and tell my dad and Murph's ma the whole story. So we did.

That's how our big First Communion day ended. One thing was for sure. The next time we went to confession, there was going to be no shortage of things to confess.

You know, to tell the truth, there never was again!

5

THE LONG WAY HOME

Our Lady of Peace School was OK, but the real fun part was going home. It wasn't just going home, it was an adventure and we stretched it out as long as we could. There were no lines of cars outside Our Lady of Peace grade school like there are today in front of most schools. Not too many people had cars during the war years and just after. I know that we didn't and neither did Murph's folks. As I have told my girls a hundred times or more, we did not get a car until I was a junior in high school and that was still a long way off.

Murph and I lived across the alley from each other. He lived at 79th and Yates and I lived at 79th and Phillips. I would come across the alley from our place in the morning, holler up the three floors for Murph and then start hiking down toward 79th. Murph was fast and he would usually catch me by the time I hit the railroad tracks, then it was down 79th, west to Chappel Avenue and into school.

In the afternoon we'd reverse the process, but for some reason it took twice as long to get home in the afternoon as to get to school in the morning. For one thing, we were more tired in the afternoon. It also took some time just to get out of school. You always had to talk to somebody about something and if it was decent weather you usually had a ledgeball game to play, or a football game in the playground behind the florist shop and greenhouse.

Then there were the basketball hoops that Father McDermott had put up on the garage despite the protests of old Monsignor Henry Friel. "Too much money,' the curmudgeon complained. "Besides, the kids will just ruin the garage doors and damage my Cadillac too." Somehow, Father Mac won this one, and the hoops stayed up.

Ledgeball, or ledge for short, was a unique local game that I doubt kids know anymore. When the area was being built up after the first World War, many of the local buildings had a one- to two-inch angled ledge at the bottom of the building about a foot or two off the ground, and our school was no exception. Decoration, I guess, because I can think of no functional reason for it whatever. When you slammed a special ball on the ledge, a simulated baseball game started. Wee Folks toy store and old Belle and Manny Lazar had the best balls: basically, the inside of a tennis ball without the fuzzy cover. When those babies hit right on the sharp, angled edge of the ledge, the result was a great fly ball. If you hit it right on the sweet spot, that ball could go over the playground fence for an obvious home run. It was a four man game, a boys' game really, no girls allowed, but I don't think they would have wanted to play anyway.

There was an infielder and an outfielder on each team and the rules were simple. Ground balls were out, no balls and strikes, errors were singles, fly-outs were outs, otherwise just get in there and slam away. Simple or not, we could easily waste a good hour playing ledge. Then it was off east down 79th to Stenson's hardware store. We were just getting started.

Mike Stenson owned the Chappel Hardware store at 2032 E. 79th. Now it helped that the Stensons were Murph's cousins on his mother's side, so we were always sure of at least a lukewarm welcome. We always looked at all the nuts and bolts. Everything was in open bins. There were no plastic bags or bubble wrap containers like today. If you needed three nuts and one bolt, that's what you bought. You didn't have to buy a bag with a dozen already prepackaged that you didn't need now and would not find when you needed one four years from now.

If it was a good day we might set up a deal to come back on Saturday and wash the windows to get a little extra money. Otherwise we just mixed up a few bins and got on our way.

Across the street was Mr. Louis Coppe's Wakeford Laundry, which was always worth a stop because sometimes his son Johnny, who was in the class behind us at OLP, would be around and that meant that there was always some mischief afoot. John was what you would call an adventurous kid. A good ballplayer and a good guy, he was always ready to get into something with that invariable grin on his face. If it was a cold day, we would go back by the big commercial dryers in the shop and warm up for the next stage home. If it was a hot day, we would go back by the dryers because it felt cooler when we got outside.

Next, we'd stop by the Whoo Dat tavern at 2055 and see who was there. Most times there would be these old Irish guys from the old country, just off the boat sounding like some turkeys gobbling away in Gaelic. Sometimes they would give us some spare change off the bar if they were in a good mood, which they usually were. This was a great place to stop in when we were selling chances for church raffles, if Father Mac hadn't already gotten up there and beat us to it. We could hear them talking about Notre Dame and Notre Dame football. The late 40s were truly golden years for the Fighting Irish and John Lujack, Johnny Lattner, Terry Brennan and our own hero, the incomparable Ziggie Czarobski. Ziggie was irrepressible, a real life of the party! Later on he opened up a great restaurant on 83rd Street down from Carl's Vienna hot dogs.

If we had our bikes, we would stop at Tiffany's service station to get some air in our tires and see if they wanted any cars washed. They usually had coffee for the customers and so on cold days we made it a point to help ourselves and warm up a bit for the next leg of the trip.

Down the block and across 79th again we went (watch out for that trolley car!). Now we were in front of our favorite tavern, Jerry's Liquors at 2222. It was a favorite because they had a big lithograph print of Custer's Last Fight, distributed by the Anheuser-Busch Brewing Company. Budweiser must have been the beer of the house but it was that picture that caught our imagination like nothing else could do. It was historically incorrect in every detail, with guys stripped and scalped already while other dismounted troopers were battling it out and old George Custer in his buckskins and two revolvers blasting away at Sitting Bull. Well, let's just say the picture had some bull indeed but that didn't bother us one bit. Every day, that picture was engraved again in our memories like nothing else. Catechism, our multiplication tables, historical facts, chores to do, anything that was important we could not remember for diddlysquat, but we could remember every detail of that lithograph and the odd thing is that in our minds, that picture was moving! It was like a movie for us. We didn't need a real theater with Errol Flynn. Like in Treasure of Sierra Madre, we didn't need no stinking movie theater. We had our own Budweiser cyclorama!

We were off again but not before we put some pennies on the trolley track in the street. Then we had to wait for the next trolley. We watched the electric trolley car get closer, rocking from side to side, bell ringing and dinging, and zap! It was like magic. Our copper pennies were now flat and elongated. We could use them for trade bait, particularly with the little kids.

We cut up the alley for a quick game of horse at Grannans. "C'mon Murph, it won't take a minute." Nobody had the court and the garage doors were open with two old beat up basketballs that had seen better days.

It didn't take too long before we got to "h-o-r" and the big guys showed up with a newer ball and they were ready to go. They were not in any mood to wait around for us.

"OK, Murph, let's stop up at the shoe store and get our feet x-rayed." This was just about a daily ritual. I'm surprised that our feet have not fallen off by now from all the green fluorescence we zapped them with. We would x-ray anything that we could think of, packages, small cartons, lunches, whatever would fit in the machine. We didn't try on any Buster Brown shoes but promised we would bring our folks in when we could. We never bought shoes there. They were just too expensive. However we would be back for one of our regular stops: the exciting world of science and magic!

Now it was over to 2303: the Crandon delicatessen. This place just smelled delicious! Fresh baked bread, Jewish delicacies, Polish ham, spicy roast beef, fresh rolls and cookies. We pooled our change saved up from days of walking and saving our carfare. It paid off in splitting a monster sweet roll. Lox and bagels, cream cheese, it was all here, but we had to go. We said so long to the pleasant Jewish clerk and slipped out the door as some other kids were coming in.

Kroger's was next. It was a regular stop, particularly if we had found any bottles to cash in. "Carry your groceries, ma'am?" we asked an older woman who we could see was struggling with three bags. She thanked us and off we went up Yates toward a three flat and wouldn't you know, she lived on the third floor. Oh well, we didn't mind the exercise and we knew our legs were getting stronger and stronger. We were looking forward to playing football someday, right down Yates at Eckersall stadium and we knew this would help us get on the way. "Thank you so much boys, she murmured as she looked in her purse for a tip. "You remind me so much of my boys a long time ago." It took a while like with all ladies, but she finally did find it. "Here's a quarter for the both of you. Can you share it?" "Yes, ma'am, no trouble, glad to help."

Off we raced down the back stairs, pushing and shoving for position. If nothing else, we had energy to burn. We had a couple last stops now so you know we were getting close to home. Murph had more chores to do so he was in more trouble than I was. He was going to have to hustle to get everything done by the time his ma came home. He still had to look after his dad but sometimes his older sister would take care of that. We had to go see Old Man Moffat at the Curtis Candy garage. We were walking down the alley one day when we met Moffat. He was a genial, elderly colored gentleman. His hair had turned white and his gnarled hands had known nothing but hard work, setting pins mostly, up at Pla-Mor lanes on the other side of Jeffery past the church. He was stooped now and frail and was working part-time at the candy garage keeping the place clean and washing trucks now and then.

"How are you young gen'mun tonight" he asked in his rich baritone. "I sure hope school is treating you all right. It's the only way to get ahead in this world, I can tell you that. You keep workin' at your books an' you'll always have a job. An' I mean a real job, not like this one." He had a radio playing somewhere in the back and the bluesy sound was amplified nicely, echoing around the support poles and up into the roof beams. "This here job ain't shit, I kin tell you dat, not good for nuthin, no-how." "Moffat, you're not having too good a day are you?" we said, trying to cheer him up a little. "Maybe you shouldn't be listening to that sad music all the time. Put on some happy music like polkas or something cheerful." "Boys," he kind of mumbled a bit, and we could tell he had been drinking a little. "You don' know how hard life can be, and happy music ain't for us colored folks." He took out a ragged bandanna and blew his nose. "I know what'll make you young gen'mun happy, yes, sir, we gotta look in the old treasure chest!" With that, he slyly motioned us to come in and opened a big wooden container filled almost to the top with out-of-date candy bars after today's deliveries.

It looked like Christmas, Halloween, and Easter all rolled into one. We had never seen so much candy in one place except maybe when the Coughlans had invited us to go the South Shore Country Club Christmas party. We were amazed and could see that old man Moffat was enjoying sharing all that loot. We stuffed our pockets to take the swag back to our fort over by the train tracks. Maybe we would share some with the little kids tomorrow. Maybe.

Next was a short stop at the Olympic Bike Shop on the corner of 79th and Phillips to look at the new models. We had done some work for the owner, "Bicycle Ben" Burstyn, so he was not disappointed to see us. He used to say that we made everybody happy: half the people by coming and half by leaving. "No work today, guys, but come back on Saturday and I might have something for you." That was OK with us as we really did have to get going. Now we had one more stop to make around the corner at the Kingston Television company. TV was brand new and so far, most of the TVs were sold to taverns for sports events. If you owned a tavern and didn't have TV or air conditioning, you were outta luck. Everybody wanted to be cool in the summer and was intrigued by television even if there was no color and the sets were 12 inch models at best. Some places tried to get a little edge by mounting a big piece of curved glass, like a magnifying glass, to the screen. That also protected the screen from thrown beer bottles when the Cubs, otherwise known as the lovable losers, blew it again.

Murph the Surf was getting edgy. "Louie, I gotta go," he said nervously. "My ma is going to kill me if she gets home and my work isn't done." We raced across the railroad tracks and headed home. I cut into our basement apartment and Murph just kept on motoring across the alley and up the three floors in world record time.

"Hi Ma," I yelled as I blew through the door, "I'm home!"

"You'd better not wake up your brother," my mom said, "or you, mister, are going to be in a real pickle!" My little dog Gyp, a golden cocker spaniel, was running around me in circles and jumping up and down like crazy. Home at last!

"What's for supper, ma," I asked quietly.

"Today's payday," mom said, "so we'll be going up to 79th Street to the Chunking Inn for dinner." This was our favorite place to go out to a real dinner in the entire neighborhood. "If you are hungry for a snack, make yourself a bread, butter and sugar sandwich."

"OK, ma, I'm hungry now."
"What took you so long to get home anyway?"
"Oh ma," I said munching on my snack sandwich, "it's a long way to walk."
"So what were you doing all that time anyway?"
"Nuthin' ma, nuthin,' there was nuthin' to do."
"What happened to your car fare?"

"Hello, family!" My dad was home. I was saved by the bell, so to speak. It was time for Chinese! Off we went to the Chunking Inn, and I got to push the buggy.

6

AN "ARFY- DARFY" DAY IN OLD JACKSON PARK

OLP was also known as the Old Ladies' Penitentiary. It was springtime, 1952, eighth grade at Our Lady of Peace school and a warm, sunny and breezy Thursday afternoon in a math class on the top floor of the old building.

Our little old Dominican nun, Sister Lucille to you, (Sister Lulu to us) was ramrod straight in front of the class, rocking slightly back and forth, tapping the maple yardstick against her hand. We groaned inwardly. Trying to stay awake was really hard, almost impossible.

We had finished lunch over an hour ago and then had a monumental game of 16 inch softball at the old "stone factory," its name taken from a long defunct concrete and masonry operation next to the railroad tracks about three blocks north of school on Chappel. All that was left of the old business was the level concrete slab foundation. It made a perfect softball diamond, particularly for the 16 inch style of play that relied on speed and constant offense in a place where you didn't have much room to move. No gloves, just an old hardwood bat, a balloon ball, and some speed and power. We had guys in the neighborhood, the big guys, who could power a new ball over the fence at old Bidwell Stadium some 300 feet, which was no mean feat!

Our unprepared hearts and minds were not into the rudimentary beginnings of algebra. We looked at the old school clock on the wall in the front of the room. The hands did not seem to have moved in 15 minutes. Time was frozen and we felt locked into a state of permanent suspension. We just wanted to be outside. Anywhere but here, and we had another six weeks of bearing the unbearable.

AN "ARFY- DARFY" DAY IN OLD JACKSON PARK

"Remembah, class," Sister Lulu said again patiently, "What evah we do to one membah of the equation, we must do to the othah." She spoke in her quiet, refined, soft Southern accent. She was from Louisville, Kentucky and had gone into the Dominicans for God only knows what reasons some fifty years earlier. She was well past retirement age and probably looking forward to going back to the old Motherhouse at St. Catherine's in Kentucky as much as we were looking forward to getting out of school.

We kept dozing off, and the maple yardstick would come down with a BANG on the miscreant's desk and he (or she) would jump about six inches in the air—eyes wide open! I whispered to Don and Bo next to me. "We've got to get out of here tomorrow. Tomorrow's Friday and I can't take any more of this. It's time to get to the park. Time for an "Arfy-Darfy" day (a Nelson Algrenism for a "Bum's Holiday").

The park. For us there was only one park—Jackson Park. Located on the northern boundary of the South Shore neighborhood, it ran from 67th Street north up to 57th Street and from Lake Michigan on the east to Stony Island Avenue on the west. It was our version of the Augusta National, Sherwood Forest, Narnia, Yellowstone Park, Oz, the Ozarks and the banks of the Mississippi River. It was our heaven on earth.

The park was the brainchild of the architect Daniel Burnham and if you want the whole story, check out, buy, borrow or steal a copy of Erik Larson's book The Devil in the White City. Burnham was the architectural genius behind the Rookery Building in the Loop and a ton of daunting building projects in Chicago in the 1890s and 1900s. His crowning glories were the Lakefront, Jackson Park and the White City. The park was built on reclaimed south side swampland next to Lake

Michigan. It was the site of the 1893 Chicago Columbian Exposition, or the Chicago World's Fair as many people called it.

You know that old Chris Columbus discovered America in 1492. The 400th anniversary was supposed to be in 1892. Even us mathematical midgets could figure that out. The extra year was due to good old Chicago politics. Somebody did not get enough arms twisted or some payoffs made. I don't know because that was "before my time" as they say. Besides, as kids, we couldn't care less. We just knew that we had the greatest playground that any kid could ever ask for.

For us kids this park had it all. It had its own beach, Jackson Park Beach, and later we watched them bring the German U-505 submarine on rollers across Lake Shore Drive to its new home alongside the Museum of Science and Industry on the north end of Jackson Park. It took all night and we even camped out in the park that night as a special treat. It was a real happening and a neighborhood party all rolled into one big special deal!

That was in the future though, and this was now. We had a great golf course in the park and our specialty was diving for golf balls in the water hazards and then selling the cleaned up balls to local hackers at a dime apiece or whatever we could get.

There was a tall golden statue of "The Republic" at one intersection for us to climb on and we had what seemed like miles of woods and bushes, until they cut them all down later as crime increased in the area. We had water—our own lagoons like some Pacific atoll. No palm trees though. Just the old midwestern cottonwoods, maples and oaks. There were loads of elms until the Dutch Elm disease hit them. The Burnham lagoons were the greatest.

They were our version of the Mississippi River and we took to them like old Tom and Huck would have. We floated homemade rafts on them, swam in them, (suits or no), and in short, treated them like our own private St. Lawrence Seaway, which was coming closer and closer to us. In 1959 it would be here.

We had the Wooded Island and the "Bridge of Sighs" they called it. It was the place where old Clarence Darrow said he would come back to on the anniversary of his final departure. Every year, on that day, people would get together on the bridge and wait for a sign from him. As far as I know none ever came and the crowd got smaller over the years until today I don't think anybody shows up. Too bad, because now Clarence probably comes back there all the time. He was a contrarian and always had a great sense of humor. I wouldn't put anything past him! His old red brick apartment building was just across from the park at

57th by the Midway Plaisance. That's probably where he goes if he comes back at all, at least in bad weather.

We even had a lawn bowling area, a green as they called it. Fenced off with a low, black chain link deal, it always had no end of old geezers rolling little balls on what looked like a golf green with that fancy Creeping Bent lawn. The old folks, men and women, all had snooty white linen outfits on with white shoes and white caps. It looked like a ton of fun; even better than horseshoes.

Later we learned to play Italian bocce ball out at Bob and Clara's Tavern in Chicago Heights. They had a fenced-in beer garden with three lighted courts and guys would play almost all night, depending on the pay-offs to the cops and how much was being bet. We didn't have white suits, but we drank some good beer there that they did not have in Jackson Park.

But I digress. It was Friday morning now and we had a big decision to make: to go or not to go. What were we going to do? We met at Moline's store across from school for the big decision. It got to be a debate. Some kids said they did not want to get in trouble so count them out. You know the type. Yesterday, they were all for it but now they weren't. Others were on the fence: maybe, maybe not. Wait and see, they said.

Among the more adventurous, the debate was over. We could not take any more algebra, catechism, or Palmer penmanship. It looked to be another beautiful spring day, the sun was coming up over the lake and our old tall tower was lit up like a lighthouse.

The park was waiting. The bus was coming. The Jeffery Express was going northbound fast and we ran across the boulevard to pick it up at 79th Street. We had to move, grabbing lunches, half-eaten bakery, chugging down soda pop and grabbing our gym bags with our towels and lunches.

We were all there, the adventurers, pirates, scouts, mountain men, what have you. The bus stopped, but not for long. This baby was headed downtown and quick. They didn't call it the Express for nothing. I looked around when we got settled in the back of the bus behind most of the grownup commuters, some of whom looked like they'd like to be going with us.

Bo was there, and Murph, me and Don, PJ, Mick, Johnny Hart, and Harry. Harry, as usual, had the hardest time trying to make up his mind. Then at the last possible second, I think somebody grabbed him and he followed the path of least resistance. Too late now boys, the die has been cast, let the good times roll! We were on our way.

The bus sped north up Jeffery and we could see, fast receding in the distance, all the kids lining up to go into school without us. Nick the janitor was sweeping up the last of the winter-borne debris. We laughed the laugh of daredevils, the laugh of the guy who has just caught the last trolley car by one hand and is hanging on for dear life, both feet parallel to the ground and swinging straight out. Consequences? What consequences? We were free for the day. Let Monday worry about itself, we were free, free, free. Thank God almighty, we were free at last.

Decision making, at least good decision making, was not yet one of our strong points. That would come later, if at all. We were finding the truth that someone once said, "It's easy to say no to your enemies; the hard part is saying no to your friends." We bounced, swayed and sat jammed together, on a CTA high, watching the kids filing into Bryn Mawr school and soon watching Mitchell's ice cream and candy shop fly by just before we hit the ICRR tracks at 71st Street. 71st Street was home to some pretty famous folks as we found out later: Marv Levy of Buffalo Bills fame; Gene Krupa, the drummer; Ezzard Charles, the great heavyweight champ; and playwright David Mamet of Glengarry Glen Ross fame. However that was not on our minds as we headed to the park.

We were speeding across 67th Street and into Jackson Park like a big green and yellow bat out of hell. The route was through the park and into Lake Shore Drive at 57th, then straight downtown nonstop along the lake to the Loop.

We had other ideas though. We weren't going downtown. Not today, thank you! There were no scheduled stops in the park. Just after we went by the tall golden statue that had been modeled after the even bigger centerpiece of the Court of Honor at the Columbian Exposition almost sixty years earlier, we made our move. We pulled the emergency cord in unison and the bus screeched to a weaving, shuddering halt on the side of the inner drive.

We were prepared of course, so it was no surprise to us. It was quite a shock though to the regular dozing and newspaper-reading passengers. It was the end of their reverie. Somebody rolled down the aisle past us and we bailed out of the rear door like a stick of paratroopers over Normandy. Luckily, most of us hit the grassy parkway, missed the light pole, and came to a rolling halt more or less intact.

We made it with only minor cuts, scrapes and bruises! I think the driver had a good idea of our modus operandi and suspected something was coming. We looked up the drive and we could see him making gestures, and even though we couldn't hear him, we suspected that he was not just wishing us good luck and bon voyage.

We hiked out across the golf course, keeping an eye out for stray golf balls that could go into our collection to sell in the coming summer. Not much luck there, since not many golfers were out yet even though it was a gorgeous, sunny, spring day.

We were making a beeline toward our first objective: the ancient rickety sailboat in the basin behind the Museum of Science and Industry up at the north end of the park. The fair authorities had commissioned three replicas of the original boats of Columbus: the Nina, Pinta, and Santa Maria. The first two were built in Chicago. The Santa Maria replica, befitting a flagship, was built in Spain and then sailed over here in 1893 for the exposition.

All three ships had been in the back basin, but over a sixty year period of decay, disuse and Chicago winters, two were no longer in existence. One was left, which was probably the Santa Maria because it was the most seaworthy. The name on the ship was long worn off and although it was listing and the sails and rigging were all but gone, it was still floating and looked like it was waiting for Errol Flynn to show up for a movie like The Sea Hawk and weigh anchor into Lake Michigan.

It took us awhile to get to the basin because of various grab-ass activities: tripping each other, tag, tackles, maulings, playing keep away with somebody's hat or lunch; in short, doing what boys of that age like to do the world over, then and now.

Then we saw it. Listing a little more than we had last seen it on a warm Indian summer day the previous October, but she still looked sort of seaworthy. The wood was almost black, with splinters all over the place but that did not deter us. We went over to the bushes and off with our shoes, pants and shirts. Last one in was a chump. First one out to the ship was the clear winner. The race was on. A couple of park district employees were taking a break, (they were always taking breaks), and they laughed at the sight of us, probably wishing they were a little younger but at least not shagging us out of there.

The only worry we had was the park district police, known affectionately as the Sparrow Cops. Patronage hacks, usually overweight, out of shape, and bone lazy, they weren't much of a deterrent. Even so, the year before we had run into one guy who thought he was Fearless Fosdick. We were swimming in one of the lagoons and he pulled out his gun on us to get us out of the water. Maybe for our own safety, but a loaded .38?

A couple of the more adventurous of us simply swam downstream underwater, came out below his squad car, and let the air out of all four tires.
He didn't bother us the rest of the summer but we didn't want to meet up with him again.

We had a blast climbing on the old ship and diving into the murky, green water. Over and over again we went with all the exuberance of cocky, glorious youth. A bevy of girls on a school field trip appeared on the museum side of the basin and we swam over to see them. We had no luck trying to convince them to join us although a couple of them looked tempted until one of their chaperones came around the corner, and that ended that!

It was getting time for lunch, so off we scampered back to the bushes, got dried off (the forward thinkers had brought towels), got our underwear wrung out and placed on the bushes to dry in the springtime sun. It was time to eat. Actually, truth be told, it was always time to eat.

We had our bag lunches and some snacks, cookies, peanuts and the like which we shared in real hobo fashion. As old Nelson Algren would have said, it was a true "Arfy-Darfy" moment, referring to being on the loose and fancy free. Just having what we called a bum's holiday. Not a care in the world.

We did need something to drink though and a couple of guys headed over to the Nike Missile base a short distance away to see if they could talk the soldiers into giving up a couple of cans of pop, or if we were lucky, a couple of cans of Meister Brau.

The Nikes had been installed in view of the cold war tensions a couple of years earlier when we were doing air raid drills in school, hiding under our desks as if that would be of any use in a hydrogen bomb attack on the Windy City. If Soviet bombers came over Lake Michigan, presumably from the north or wherever the Soviet Union was, they would be dead ducks, according to local wisdom.

We were not so sure about all that, but when the guys came back they had three or four cans of cold pop. We figured if our troops were passing out candy and treats to the kids in Korea, they certainly couldn't refuse some of their own kids right here. After all, who were they fighting for? Now we really had it made, with cold pop to be shared, sandwiches, and some snacks. This was pig heaven indeed. Murph turned to Bo and said, "Hey Bo, it doesn't get any better than this!" That summed it up for all of us.

Now it was time to get on the move again. This was too good of a day to go inside the museum itself. We reserved that for rainy days or days so hot and humid that we got relief just being in the cool, comfortable wonderland. Not today though. We headed for the riding stables on Stony Island to see the horses. Sometimes, if we were lucky and the stable hands were in a good mood on a slow day, they let us take the horses out for a short ride, keeping a good eye on us all the way.

No such luck today. The hands were not in a particularly good mood but they did let us feed the horses and run some water in their drinking pails. It smelled good in the barns: a mix of feed, hay, muck, and sunshiny warmth, insects buzzing around and the wonderful smell and warmth of the horses themselves. We were now in horse heaven.

All of a sudden, a group of snooty rich kids showed up with adults. All of them must have been regulars because they had all the right stuff: velvet covered helmets, jodhpurs, shiny leather boots and riding crops. They made us look kind of weak in our wet jeans, khakis and ripped and tattered gym shoes. They looked at us like we had just been mucked out of a stall and were getting ready to be shoveled out back into the manure pile. All the horses were saddled now and the stable hands were occupied so it was time to go. We thought about making a grand exit and causing a commotion with the few firecrackers we had, along with jabbing a couple of the horses with the pitchforks and create our version of Buffalo Bill's Wild West Show. The show had played just outside these grounds in 1893 during the Exposition where Hyde Park High School is today. Luckily, cooler heads prevailed, and we left quietly without causing any scene. We really didn't want to burn any bridges. It was going to be a long summer and we wanted to come back on good terms. There would be other days and other times.

We headed south toward home, noticing that the sky was getting darker and a big spring storm was rolling in from the west. There was rolling thunder and a bolt of lightning! It was time to get going.

Too late. We had gotten no further than a quarter mile or so, and the sky opened up with a deluge that made us wish we had stayed at the museum. We were soaked in minutes, even after getting under some fair sized trees. Then the lightning let loose and exploded and cracked all around us so we thought we'd better get moving again. We laughed to think about those rich snoots, probably from the University of Chicago Lab School, getting soaked out on the bridle trails. That cheered us up a little bit. Maybe they weren't as bright as they thought they were. Common sense does count for something, we thought, even though we were not using too much of it either.

Just ahead, through a lightning bolt, we could see a park shelter. It was big and open on all four sides with picnic benches inside. It looked darn good now and it was all we had so we cut up that way as fast as we could.

As we got closer we saw two older men already in the shelter. Even from a distance, these two dorks did not look right. We had heard about perverts in the parks preying on young kids but right now we had no other choice. Besides, there were eight of us and while we weren't invincible we felt that we could take care of any situation that popped up.

Sure enough, they gave us a kind queer welcome that sent messages up and down my back. They had clean dry towels and offered to dry us off but we weren't buying into that. Finally they just threw them to us and we just dried off as quick as we could. We gave them a strong message that we were not going to play their game and that we had enough strength, speed and moxie to take care of them very handily. It was now down to "you leave us alone and we'll leave you alone"—a real Mexican standoff.

After about fifteen minutes, although it seemed an hour, the storm lifted a bit. There was still thunder and lightning but not much rain now. All of a sudden we had company and it wasn't the kind we were usually looking for. A gang of young Negros, most in some kind of raggedy baseball uniforms, started to crowd into the shelter. They were laughing and jiving around, shadow boxing with each other and looking us over real good. They couldn't quite figure out who our queers were or what they were doing here, but they were eyeing them warily. Some of the uniforms had the team name on them. They were the Mighty MoJos from east 47th Street. They had their bats, mitts and balls and they were older, bigger, stronger and faster. We were in trouble.

We tried some negotiation first. Our best negotiator was Mick. Slick Mick. His dad owned a laundry in the neighborhood and he had been working there since kindergarten. Mick offered to set up a game for next week. That didn't get very far. Their captain, a surly, lighter complexioned kid with an attitude was saying, "Whafo we wanna play you dudes fo? You ain't got sheeeet!" His buddies roared and began dancing around us singing some Motown melody like we were in some kind of echo chamber. You had to hand it to them, they had rhythm, but we were getting the blues. Then I noticed that the four bigger boys with the bats had moved out to surround us and we were ringed in by the Mighty MoJos with no exit.

To give Mick credit, he did not back down an inch. He showed absolutely no fear and he was a pretty good sized rangy kid, and a smooth infielder. Of all of us kids he was the only one that could have played pro ball. His dad had other ideas, however, and so Mick took over the laundry business instead.

We could see that out of nowhere a number of them had produced automobile antennas ripped off various cars in the park. At least two others had switchblades. Mick kept talking though and the leader just kept getting cockier: "You dudes ain't got nuthin'. Whatchu got, huh?"

Luckily, nobody had noticed that little Johnny Hart, master of the dirty joke, who could have done standup comedy with his stuff, had slipped away. He was the smallest of all of us and I was glad to see that he had avoided the beating that was surely coming.

Suddenly, we heard strange sounds and noises. It sounded like shovels crunching in gravel: crunch,

crunch, clack, clack crunch. Then I saw Johnny come smiling around the corner of the shelter. Everybody stopped and Captain MoJos's mouth dropped open. Behind Johnny was almost the entire Mount Carmel football team in their old practice jerseys. The Champs of Chicago for the previous two years, in 1950 and 1951 they had compiled a fantastic record. This team would take the City Championship again this year in 1952.

A good number of them, Bill Durham, big Danny DelGrosso, Leon Dourlet, and Bill Drew were all from our OLP grade school and knew Johnny. They had been practicing in Jackson Park for spring ball and were not in the best of moods. They were muddy, soaking wet, bruised and pissed off.

They wasted no time. Danny picked up Captain MoJo and threw him across the shelter into a heap against a support post. The football players grabbed anybody who had a weapon and tackled them, picked them up, knocked them down again. They took off their helmets and swung them like maces. The Mighty MoJos were wiped out, most running out of the park back toward 47th Street. Blood was everywhere and things were over before they knew it. They were screaming epithets and bloody murder but they were beaten and beaten good. Our own two old queers were hugging each other and laughing and we were all getting our kicks in while we could. Finally, all the Mighty MoJos were gone, dragging their captain with them. They were the Mighty Mopes, as it turned out. Everybody was backslapping and shaking hands. We were ecstatic.

You could have made a good movie about it: "Remember the Caravan!" Even the Carmel coaches who had come up by this time were laughing. Our local heros from the neighborhood had saved our butts. We would be grateful forever. The storm was over and it was time for us to head home. Battered, bruised, and sunburned, it was worth it for one day of freedom; a real Arfy-Darfy day in every way!

We stumbled across the park like a group of Bataan death march survivors and headed back home in bright sunshine again. No 'grabass' now like in the morning. We caught a bus on Stony Island and headed south to 79th where we would transfer to the #79 and head back east. I got off at Constance right by our favorite store, Wee Folks toys. It was Mom and Pop Lazar's gem of magic, toys and dreams and the Jewish owners named their place after the Irish "little people." Only in America. I didn't stop in today though. I could hardly walk and I had two blocks to go to our place at 7711 Constance.

My mom, bless her heart, was home and in good shape. I found out years later that the school had called about my absence but she never let on. "How was school today?" she asked with a little smile. "Oh great, Ma. Just the usual, you know," I said, trying to be nonchalant. "Well, good for you, but you look like you've been through a steel mill. Get cleaned up quick. We're going out for Chinese tonight—your favorite place, the Chunking Inn."

I took off for my room and kind of laid low the rest of the weekend, not wanting to think a whole lot about Monday. It would be here soon enough.

Monday morning dawned bright and clear again. The eight of us met together at Harry's house and trudged together up to school looking altogether like the so-called, "Black Sox" who were banned from baseball for life after the 1919 World Series for gambling and conspiracy to throw the World Series. There was nothing to do now but get up to school and face the medicine.

Just as we got up to school and into the playground, Jim Sherman and Terry Tobin, the "brains" of our class, came running up with the news.

"Guess what, you guys," they exclaimed breathlessly. "You missed it—we didn't have any school on Friday. There was a surprise party for Monsignor Friel's anniversary and retirement and the Bishop was here and Little Oscar and the Weinermobile and Bud Bowman and we had some great food: hot dogs, hamburgers, the works. We had all the ice cream and candy we could eat."

We looked at each other a bit ruefully. "You've got to be kidding, right?"

They were not kidding. We had sure picked the wrong day to take off. Now we still had to pay the proverbial piper. When we walked into class, Sister Lulu sent us to the principal's office to see Sister DePorres. When she got done with us we had to work with Nick the janitor every night after school for the next three weeks to clean up around the school and the playground.

"We knew where you boys had gone," she said seriously, "and we had Nick keep an eye on you all the time. You know that this is your last year here and we want you to go through graduation. Please remember that next year you will all be in high school and everything really counts then. There can be no more of this little boy behavior, you are getting to be real men now and don't forget it!"

So we never did forget it. At least until the next time.

7

ALLEYCATS AND THE "BIG BANG" THEORY

"It isn't hard to love a town for its greater and its lesser towers, its pleasant parks or its flashing ballet. Or for its broad and bending boulevards, where the continuous headlights follow, one dark driver after the next, one swift car after another, all night, all night and all night. But you never truly love it till you can love its alleys too. Where the bright and morning faces of old familiar friends now wear the anxious midnight eyes of strangers a long way from home."

- From Nelson Algren's Chicago: City on the Make

When we were growing up in the '40s and '50s, the alleys in Chicago were very important and interesting places. At least they were on the south side. I don't know what they were like on the north side at all. We never went to the north side. Maybe they didn't even have alleys. One thing for sure, they did not have streets with numbers. Not like our big streets anyway: 47th Street, 63rd Street, 71st Street, and our main street,

79th Street. You measured your independence by the numbers that your folks laid on you. "Don't go past 75th Street," they'd say. Or, "Don't you dare go past 79th Street! Or else!" The "else" was not usually spelled out. They wanted plenty of flexibility for consequences.

The paved concrete alleys were not much more than a big truck wide. Two cars could never get by side by side. The alleys were the lifeblood of our economy. They seemed to belong to the service people.

The milkman used them every day but Sunday. We woke up on sleepy Saturdays to the rhthymic clip-clop clip-clop of weary horses' hooves.

Maybe it was the war and the end of the Depression, plus the fact that the auto industry was frozen for war production and gas was rationed, but we had a good number of horse-drawn wagons then. There were ragtag wagons collecting rags. "Rags here, raggedy rags." "All rags here!" Singsong.

There were weary blackened wagons for coal. The burley ice men had wagons pulled by equally burley draft horses and always had chunks of ice for us on the hot Chicago summer days.

The junk man had a nondescript wagon pulled by an equally nondescript dray horse. Then there was the scissors and knives sharpener with his smaller wagon with pots and pans hanging on the sides, adding to the din and musical cacophony of clangs and bangs with the loud calls: "Scissors to sharpen. Hey-hey, get your knives ready for Sunday!"

In spite of this passing of an era, we still had an assortment of motley old trucks and cars limited by the strict rationing of gas and oil. There were some coal trucks, grocery delivery panel trucks, and other workmen's trucks of all kinds: electricians, plumbers and the like. Tradesmen.

Beyond all this commercial traffic, the alleys served another valuable function for us kids. Every block had at least one, and some two or more, wooden basketball backboards and hoops attached to the garage roofs. All were nominally set at ten feet high, but this was negotiable. Some baskets were at 10 feet, one inch or more. Some never made it up to ten feet and others, adjusting for the relative height of the owner and his buddies, were set at the rational height of six to eight feet.

The rules were simple. First: no girls allowed. Period. Second: no mopes allowed. Whoever owned the court took the ball out first. This was straight two on two basketball. Fouls were not called unless blood was drawn and then the worst that happened was a grudging, "aw, shit!" turnover. No foul shots were needed.

It was all action. Action was the name of the game. No finesse necessary. No slugging or kicking but everything else was fair play. Alley ball was no place for sissies!

You played to 21 with each basket worth a point, and you had to win by two. Some of the games would go neck and neck, back and forth to 35 points, 50 points or more. The classic record setter at Hank Grannon's was just over 100 points with the game called because of darkness and rain after two and a half hours!

The regular schedule was from early mornings (on Saturdays, holidays and holy days) until dusk, with breaks for lunch, supper and totally inclement weather.

This was really no-holds-barred basketball. There was not enough room to be fancy and as soon as the ball was in play from backing up and kicking the opposite side garage door, the heat was on. This was muscular basketball at its best – or worst – and the winning team could hold the court, sometimes all afternoon. The biggest interruptions were cars trying to get in or out of their garages or deliverymen coming and going, some of whom even stopped and got into the game for a little break from their job.

We spent a lot of time playing alley ball in all kinds of weather. Snow slowed us up a bit until we got the court shoveled off or we decided to go out in the neighborhood and look for sidewalks to shovel for 25 or 50 cents, maybe even a buck if we got lucky. Then it was off to Moline's at 79th and Jeffery for greasy Mo-burgers, sweet rolls, Cokes and candy. Carb loading, they would call it today. Pigging out was what we called it.

In point of fact, the alleys of South Shore were probably like the canals of Venice to the water rats in Italy. The alleys were our lifelines and our shortcuts. Especially if we were walking down the street and spotted our local bully Considine and his cronies coming our way, the alleys saved us. If we saw a group of girls from school moving towards us, we would cut through the nearest gangway, escape into the next alley as fast as we could and disappear like Houdini.

We ran in the alleys, we roller skated in them, played a form of trash can roller hockey and in short, used them like a private conduit to go wherever we wanted whenever we wanted.

Unlike the others in my neighborhood, I didn't have a basketball backboard or hoop on our garage. I had something even more interesting. We lived across the alley behind Murray Humphreys' home at 77th and Bennett. His nickname was the Camel (from the "Hump") and he was one of the top-ranking mobsters in the Chicago syndicate. He was the model for Tom Hagen, the Consigliere in the Godfather trilogy. Only he wasn't Italian. He was a very low profile kind of guy, handsome with dark wavy hair, and a dapper, well dressed man who usually wore a camel hair overcoat in cooler weather. He was never alone, usually accompanied by his assistant Ralph Pierce and a bodyguard or two. At times he would be with his beautiful second wife, Jeanne Stacy or his daughter, Llewella, from his first marriage to Clemi Humphreys, who was the bookkeeper for the mob. Humpheys had moved into the South Shore neighborhood in 1936 and took over the outfit when Big Al Capone died in prison in 1947.

Because there was so much traffic to and from the house, which was surrounded by a barbed wire-crowned chain link fence that was electrified at the top, he had installed quite an arrangement. There was a tall reinforced chain-link gate into the yard from the alley, which was locked at all times. Next to the gate and built into the fence was a series of steel boxes, each one bigger than the last.

The big one on the bottom was for groceries, the middle one was a real refrigerator (a lot of us still had ice boxes), and the top one was a steel-encased telephone, the key to which was given only to the most trusted vendors to call the house after the delivery of items. Upon receiving the call, a housekeeper, or bodyguard if the housekeepers were otherwise engaged, would trudge outside and bring in the delivery.

It was the July 4th weekend and we were bored. The neighborhood parade was over and the ROTC cadets and band from South Shore High School were long gone. Our baseball game was over, and now we were antsy. It was hot, dull and humid and we were restless. What could we do now?

A car came down the alley and pulled up to a screeching halt in front of us. At least the brakes worked! It was the famous "Dominguezmobile," a '30s-era jalopy that the Dominguez brothers, along with the

Talamonte boys, had cut the top off with a welding torch and worked on for weeks down the alley from us. It was low, rumbling and really kind of goofy looking, but it was theirs and it had been modified into one heavy duty muscle car, fast and dangerous. It was also packed with young teens ready for just about anything. This was usually a recipe for disaster. Greetings were exchanged, both profane and cheerful. "Hey, you dummies," was one of the nicer ones. "Why not get off your butts and see what we got" they yelled. "We just got back from the fireworks factory in Indiana!"

They lifted the trunk lid that had been fastened with somebody's old leather belt and a bicycle chain. We all gathered around to look at case after case of illegal fireworks that somebody's older brother had bought at the infamous Aladdin's Fireworks in Munster, Indiana.

The cases were carefully unloaded in the Sheehan's garage. We all sat around trying to think of what to do with the stash. Somebody thought of climbing up the Our Lady of Peace tower and bombing everything that moved on Jeffery Boulevard below, but cooler heads prevailed.

"Hey," said Tommy Carpenter, who would be known forever after this evening as 'Tom the Bomb," "I know. My ma has saved up a ton of Maxwell House coffee cans—the big ones. Why don't we take all these babies apart, take the powder out, and make a real big firecracker?"

We didn't think about it at the time, but "big firecracker" became a kind of euphemism, whatever a euphemism was, for a bomb. Tommy came back shortly with two huge coffee cans and we got to work. All of a sudden we were not bored or restless anymore. It got real exciting fast and we got real busy. We were on a roll now.

It took a couple of hours with everybody helping to dissect each firecracker, cherry bomb, Roman candle and M-80. Finally we had the powder out and into the coffee cans. "Good to the last drop!" one wag laughed with glee. Somebody else got the bright idea to line the cans with large nails pilfered from his old man's garage down the alley. "Why not?" we thought. "This'll make it more interesting! I wonder what'll happen?"

It was getting dark when we finished our job. Tommy thought we should name the two containers. Smitty said he had an idea for the two "automatic" bombs:
"Fat Man and Little Boy" (or was it the other way around?).

"You dumb shit,' roared the big guys. "that's the atomic bomb, dummy"
"Well," responded Smitty in defense, "they went off automatically, didn't they? "Smitty," they laughed. "You are dumber than dirt and sadder than a bag of rocks!"

This went on for a couple of minutes until the big guys got tired of it and the conversation turned to the proposed target. Where were we going to set these small bombs off?

Some guys voted for the little Chinese laundry on 78th Street all by itself over east in a residential neighborhood. It made some cockeyed sense because the Chinese were fighting our guys in Korea at the time and this would somehow pay them back for the hammering we were taking there. Others voted for the new synagogue over on 79th and Yates Boulevard. That got nixed because some of the guys had been to the open house when it was finished and had had a good time and a lot to eat. Besides, nobody wanted to go a mile east. Wasn't there some closer target?

The idea seemed to hit us all at once. Of course! Why didn't we think of it before? Murray Humphreys' place. He was a crook, everybody said, although none of us knew exactly what he did. One guy said that his old man knew for a fact that Humphreys had somehow been involved in a string of gangland murders all over the city. "Something about unions," one guy added.

That was it then. We had a consensus. Murray Humphreys, aka "the Camel," would get the hit. And the delivery boxes would be the perfect target. The best thing was that if and when the cops showed up, they wouldn't want to get involved with what looked like a mob hit and would not pursue us any too hard. It was a done deal and it was getting dark. Other fireworks were going off sporadically all over the neighborhood. It was time to go.

As quietly as we could, a small group of us took both cans, now attached with fuses somebody had gotten from an old construction site, and we snuck through the darkening shadows like a bunch of commandos attacking a German headquarters. Whatever else we may have lacked, imagination wasn't one of them.

We carefully placed both cans on top of the big box and next to the refrigerator. One crazy kid we called "No Toes" Callahan (because he had been standing too close to an IC train or streetcar when he was a little kid) was one of the most daring kids around, so we nominated him to place the cans. Besides, we reasoned, he had already lost his toes, so what if he lost his fingers or his hand. Tough toenails!

Everything was ready. The die was cast when suddenly the back porch lights went on. We froze. They were on about a minute but no one came out into the back yard. We could breathe again. The matches came out of Tommy's pocket and were passed over to "No

Toes." Again everything got deathly quiet. Maybe this wasn't such a good idea after all. Too late. Couldn't chicken out now. "No Toes" scraped the wooden match on the concrete alley surface. We were startled at the size of the flare and the acrid smell of sulphur. The fuses started to spark and sizzle. We didn't have much time now. We took off down the alley to a designated hiding spot.

We had almost gotten to our hideout when we first felt, then heard, a terrific KA-BOOM and then the echo: ka-boom, boom, boom.

The "big bang" theory was in fact real. We could see fragments of metal and barbed wire fencing sailing through the air, outlined by a rising moon. Our own "midnight eyes" grew wider in disbelief. The first thing I really could focus on was the fact that most of our garage door was missing. Gone. Vanished. A black, smoking, gaping hole.

We did not own a car so I wasn't too worried about that. But I suddenly thought of my great uncle Ed's new '51 Olds 88. What had happened to that? Uh-oh...I was a goner.

I thought about my cousin Gil. Gilbert Lewis had dropped out of Fenger High School in Roseland and joined the Army. At age 16, he found himself in the middle of Chinese mass attacks and somehow survived to become a Chicago cop. If the army took him, maybe there was a chance they would take me too. But at thirteen, even being big for my age ("husky," they called it then), there wasn't much chance of passing for 17 or 18.

Actually, there was a traveling circus in town. Maybe that was the answer. I had loved reading Toby Tyler years earlier and still thought it would be kind of romantic to get out of Chicago and see the country while feeding the elephants.

Now reality beckoned. Lights were coming on all over the neighborhood. Humphreys' house was lit up like a Christmas tree and we could see figures in and out of the shadows running back and forth. In our imaginations, we could also see the Tommy guns and sawed-off shotguns being waved in our direction.

We could hear some of the neighbors talking about they were afraid this was going to happen someday. "Good riddance," went the theme, "we knew this was going to happen. Just a matter of time is all. Sure hope our kids are OK."

"What about his wife and daughter, are they all right?" "Yeah,"said someone in the dark, "I just saw them, and they looked OK." "Damn gangsters anyway," he muttered. "Why don't they just go back to Cicero or River Forest? We don't need 'em here." We heard the wail of police sirens and fire engines. Car 147 was on the way. It was time to say goodbye.

We slipped through a gangway and headed down another alley toward 79th Street, toward Molines and sanctuary. It was time for some greasy MoBurgers and some Jays potato chips and maybe a Green River pop or two. Mo's was a real hideaway for us. It was a respite from the stress of Our Lady of Peace school, which was just across Jeffery Boulevard. It was run by Mom and Pop Moline, who were occasionally helped out by their (all of 30 something) son, Ken. The older Molines were Russian Jews who had somehow gotten out of the Soviet Union and away from Uncle Joe before the war. This little store was a real Mom and Pop special and it was a haven for us as long as we did not start cussing too much or start roughhousing with each other and scare the paying customers away.

In the back of the store they had a blackened grill which was always going, loaded with fried onions and ready for their infamous Mo burgers. When you put your order in for these greasy specials, they would just go to the cooler and take out a number of prepared balls of meat mixed with ketchup, more onions, and spices.

These would be slapped on the hot grill and smushed down with an antique metal spatula that might have come on the boat from Russia. We are probably paying a price for all the burgers we consumed and I suspect that some of us have paid "the ultimate price" as well. In those days though, we did not know or care about cholesterol, calories or saturated fat. Ignorance was truly bliss!

We were breathing hard when we got in and put in our order. Ken was on duty that night as Mr. and Mrs. "Mo" wanted to see the fireworks show downtown on the lakefront. "Hey guys, whatcha been up to?" asked Ken, who was always cheerful, happy-go-lucky and just plain glad to be in South Shore instead of St. Petersburg.

"Oh, nothin' much Mr. Ken," replied Tom the Bomb, "just hangin' out."

"You guys never just "hang out" Ken laughed. "You're always on the make –or the take – whichever comes first."

"Awwww, Mr. Ken", said Tommy, "You make it sound like we're always doin' somethin' evil—maybe we'll just have to take our business elsewhere, over to the Pla-Mor lanes."

Ken smiled knowingly, "You guys been barred over there so many times, they don't even let you set pins no more!" He was right. We really didn't have too many options.

"So what'll it be, gentlemen, and I am using the term loosely," he smiled. We got our orders in and grabbed some Mrs. Jays potato chips for a snack along with some day-old Mrs. Hackel's sweet rolls. This was special feast for a special day: the good old Fourth of July.

"By the way," Ken lowered his voice and looked around behind him, "The cops have been in looking for you. 147's been up here twice now trying to get a lead on the bombing at the Camel's house!" "Holy, Jeeze," we protested, "we didn't do nothin'. Dam' cops." "They didn't say you did" said Ken. "They were just wanting to know if you saw anything, that's all. They know that you guys hang out in the alley behind the Camel's place. You're always workin' on cars or shootin' baskets."

"Hey," we hollered, "keep an eye on them burgers, they're startin' to burn! And put some cheese on six of them. Please."

Ken smiled another knowing smile. "Anything you want, guys, anything you want. The customer is always right, old Marshall Field used to say. And my folks always say the same thing."

We got our bottles of pop from the old red cooler and settled in for a well-deserved feast. All of a sudden, the little store's windows began to reflect flashing red lights, lots of red lights. We heard the screech of brakes, and then a siren wound down outside. It got deathly quiet. We looked at each other. Car 147 was here. We were trapped.

When the two officers walked in we were busy chomping away on our burgers. We knew one of them, Mike Danaher who was from the neighborhood, but the other one was a complete stranger. "About time you boys got up here," Danaher said. The other cop must be a rookie. He left everything up to Mike but continued to eye us all with a suspicious look, "malocchio" as our Italian buddies would have called it: the evil eye.

"We didn't do nothing, officer," cried Smitty, catching a swift knee in the butt from "No-Toes." "Didn't say you did," the rookie said quietly. "Did any of you see anything strange at Murray Humphreys' place tonight?"

"His daughter had her clothes on," whispered Tommy with a grin. "What was that?" asked Officer Danaher. "Did you say something, wise-ass?" Tommy wiped the smirk off his face and looked down at the floor sheepishly. "No sir, nothing."

"No-Toes" could be pretty smooth and slick when the situation called for it. Often missing pieces of his memory, he was determined to get it right this time. "We were playing basketball by the house earlier tonight and a strange car went by a couple of times, casing the place out."

"Now we're gettin' someplace, boys," the rookie chimed in. "What did you see?" "No-Toes" paused for a couple seconds like he was straining to bring back a long-forgotten part of his memory box.

"Four guys, dark coats, fedoras, sunglasses. They went around the block twice. I remember them for busting up our game. They weren't real polite about it either. Had a kind of bad attitude about 'em."

"Anything else? What kind of car were they driving?" "No-Toes" was an expert on automobile identification. His old man owned a used car dealership in South Chicago and he had been around cars all his life.

"1936 Oldsmobile, black. Clean and well taken care of."

Why the hell he gave them a description of my grandfather's car I'll never know. When I asked him later he just said that he had always liked that particular car, especially the topless hood ornament.

What if my grandfather Joe Hannan decided to come back to his old house and visit his family, either us or his brother? I decided that "No-Toes" was just plain nuts. Crazy.

"What time did you boys finish playing basketball and decide to come up here for your party?" The rookie didn't say much, but didn't want to let us off the hook. I started to tell him, when behind us, without any of us hearing her come in, was Sister Ann, our seventh grade teacher. She was ferocious, strict, and absolutely no-nonsense all the way. Here she was in our local hangout looking for all the world like an overweight penguin in her full black and white habit with the almost floor-length rosary beads at her side, attached to a shiny leather belt. We all nearly fell over in shock. We were really cooked now! Grilled like a Mo-burger.

But, miracles happen. "Hello boys," she said to all of us, including the cops. We later found out that Mike Danaher had had Sister Eunice Ann in seventh grade a decade ago and she had nailed him to a wall one time for grabbing the butt of one of the prettier girls in class. The girl didn't really complain, but by the time Sister Eunice Ann got done with Danaher, his butt was pretty sore and red from ruler marks.

"I wanted to thank you boys for helping me with the cake sale tonight." She smiled, really kind of a grimace, but about all the smile you were ever going to get from Sister Ann. "A fundraiser," she said to the cops. "We do it every big holiday for the missions."

"So they were with you, Sister?" The rookie was talking more now. Maybe because Danaher was in a kind of shock at seeing his old nemesis again. "Yes, they were, officer," she said, piously, "and good boys they are too. I don't know what I'd have done without them tonight."

Ken Moline said, "Yes sir, these boys have never been a bit of trouble in here either. Always glad to have them! Real young gentlemen."

We looked around. Did they mean us?

The car 147 crew was looking deflated and surprised, as if the air had been suddenly let out of their tires and they just discovered a set of nuns with ice picks surrounding all four wheels in the middle of the night in a not too good neighborhood. "Well, thank you Sister for all your information. If we need anything more we'll let you know. Boys, it's time to be getting home now, hurry along."

When we got back to our own turf it was quiet again. The fire engines were long gone and so were the cops. The Camel's house was dark now and quiet. It looked like nothing had happened at all.

Had it all been a dream? Maybe a "Fig Newton" of our imagination, as my old man used to say? Then I saw our garage doors. They didn't exactly exist, at least not like they used to. Also, my great-uncle's car was a real mess. The trunk was dented and the paint was blistered. We got ready to face the music.

Fortunately, things worked out very well, all things considered. The insurance man had come right over from down the block and assured Uncle Ed his car would be taken care of, telling him to bring it to the Spitfire garage up on Stony Island the next afternoon. My folks were pleased to learn that the garage doors would be taken care of as well.

The cops had told them and everybody that it must have been gang-related. Maybe just a scare tactic, who knew? Best to just get on with things as long as nobody was hurt.

And nobody was. At least not yet.

Well, we had the luck of the Irish on that one, I'd say. Or, as the Camel would say, the luck of the Welsh. In between times until he died in 1965 at Marina City ("an unnatural death" said Mike Royko of the Chicago Daily News, "in bed!"), he always led a quiet, low profile life, trying not to attract undue attention to himself, his family or his operations. He was not Sam Giancana. His daughter Llewella later fell in love with an Italian movie star and changed her name to Luella Brady.

Mr. and Mrs. "Mo" retired and Ken took over the place until the neighborhood collapsed after Manny Lazar was shot and killed in a robbery attempt gone bad at the "new" Wee Folks store on 79th Street in 1970. Ken was lucky and sold Mo's to McDonalds because the guy who owned all the franchises on the south side did not want any competition.

Sr. Eunice Ann went down to the Dominican Mother House in Kentucky and later we heard, though none could prove it, was committed to a mental health center.

Tommy Carpenter, aka "Tom the Bomb" later burned Downey's coal yard to the ground in a million dollar fire that also took out old Bidwell Stadium, former home of the Bluebirds girls softball team that played there all during the war. He was caught and sentenced to the Boy's Reformatory at St. Charles, Illinois. He never reformed.

"No-Toes" Callahan sold his old man's auto dealership and made it big in Chicago real estate, particularly in commercial property in the Loop. They say that he and his family had a bundle of inside clout from the Daleys but I don't know anything about that.

Sgt. Mike Danaher became a police lieutenant, later made captain and became the head of Grand Crossing station. Our own Grand Crossing! Home of car

147. He retired and invested in Sam Rinella's night club on the north side. Sam was shot to death gangland style in front of his home at 78th and Chappell right behind Our Lady of Peace in December of 1951.

All the altar boys made a monster tip on that funeral, enough to take their families out to a good dinner at Joe Biggley's restaurant on 79th Street. Or, maybe it was Alexanders. Anyway, it was a high class joint—definitely not Moline's. The rest of us grew up, went to high school, or college in some cases, got married, had families, moved away, tried to take care of our folks, and eventually retired and passed on. Just like everybody else.

8

THE GOOD WAR

We were born just after the Depression and before the big war, the one Studs Terkel called "The Good War." We grew up surrounded by the military operations of World War II. As young children we heard very little on the radio or in conversation that was not somehow connected to one battlefront or another.

We saw the flags in the windows with the blue stars for sons or daughters in the service or gold stars for those who had lost their lives. We heard stories about the older guys who had gone into harm's way from South Shore and Our Lady of Peace. We listened to our priests, Fathers McDermott, Jordan or Friel, praying every Sunday and Holy Day for the safety of our soldiers, sailors and airmen serving overseas or still in this country, training to go into battle soon.

We followed the progress of our forces and our allies around the world in colored maps in the newspapers as the war progressed. We saw pictures of the carnage in Life magazine and others all around us, at the doctor's offices, libraries, or offices. We saw the ROTC cadets from South Shore High School as they marched every day on the streets around the school, Bennett, Constance, and 77th Street.

We were in awe of the military on the streets as they came home on leaves or got a furlough after basic training or boot camp. We often saw military police from the US Fifth Army, which was partly headquartered in Hyde Park and assisted the Chicago cops in patrolling because of the number of police officers on active duty.

Around the huge Chicago Vocational School, old CVS, at 87th and Anthony, we could see the stacks of F4F fighters, their wings folded up as they waited to be worked on in a crash training program for airframe mechanics. If we went downtown, we could see the simulated aircraft carrier off Navy Pier, an old tub with a wooden deck built on top, training carrier pilots like our own Commander "Butch" O'Hare. A number of old planes are still out there off the pier, underwater and close to the water filtration plant.

My dad was not in the service because he had a number of deferments, but he did work in war production all during the conflict. He was a machinist for Mall Tool Company at 79th and South Chicago where it crosses Stony Island Avenue. They were making chain saws for the Sea Bees and other combat engineering operations. Mall's power tools are collector's items today, and if you can find them they are probably still working.

I will never forget the day that the Marines came to our street, South Phillips Avenue, to dedicate a little park right about where 80th Street would have gone through but didn't because of some long forgotten city planners' snafu. I was sick as the proverbial dog with some childhood ailment or other. Lucky for me, though, we lived in a basement apartment with good size windows right at street level. My baby brother Donnie and I shared a bedroom that looked out at the gangway between our building and the next three story building.

I was really disappointed that I couldn't go to the dedication and I was feeling quite sad when I looked up and could see a Marine honor guard in dress blues and white gloves, all spit and polish, from the Great Lakes Naval Training Center. I had no problem hearing the drill sergeant barking out the commands in our narrow gangway. The sound was magnified and the crash of the rifle butts echoed and reverberated through the tunnel-like passageway between apartment buildings.

I simply couldn't believe it. My dad had asked them to come down and visit his sick kid. The Marines had landed and landed in front of my bedroom. Baby Donnie was wide-eyed and started crying because of all the noise and the commotion. My mom came in and comforted him and we all sat and watched the sharpest troops you could ever imagine. Soon they were done with their classy drill routine and the sergeant gave the order to fall out. The Marines crowded down around my window to talk to me while my dad went into the back of the basement and got bottles of cold Green River pop for the Marines. We were lucky. Mr. Mieslowski upstairs was the local distributor for Green River and we always had cases of it around, to the amazement of the rest of the neighborhood.

Thanks to my dad, if I could not go to the parade, the parade could come to me. I was in seventh heaven and was the envy of all the other kids in the neighborhood, particularly the Coughlin brothers, TJ and Dick, and Tom Murphy.

The whole neighborhood mobilized for the war effort. We had victory gardens in the prairie behind us. We worked all spring and summer to keep those plots weeded and watered in the hot Chicago summer. In early fall we would have a corn roast and the whole block would be there. It was like a small town festival to us.

We had our own air raid wardens, Mr. Langston and Mr. Styer. You'd better have your lights out during an air raid drill or they would issue you a ticket. There was no fooling around in those days because people respected authority. They had white civilian defense armbands and steel World War I helmets painted white. It was the real deal, because you could never tell when those German or Japanese bombers would come in high over 79th Street and try to wipe out our victory gardens.

We kids were mobilized too. We collected scrap metal up and down local alleys and then brought it to the Nicholson's scrap yard pickup point by the railroad tracks. We collected everything: old batteries, pots and pans, paper bundles, bottles, you name it. Who used it and what it was used for, nobody ever told us. It didn't matter. We were sure we were doing our part to win this war.

We built forts out on the prairies away from the gardens nearer the railroad tracks that carried coal twice a day from the yards somewhere west to the steel mills on Lake Michigan in South Chicago. Typically, our forts were just one man (or two boy) foxholes but we could get very elaborate. The top of the line model was a classic fort, a bunker really, by the train tracks.

It was deep, five feet or more and reinforced with railroad ties for support beams and side wall supports. The top was 4x8 reinforced plywood, nailed down and covered with reinforced concrete. This thing could have taken a direct hit from a 500 pound bomb. It had two separate sections and the larger one even had a stove. We were ready for any contingency and practically lived out there all summer. Maybe it's still there.

The largest single military presence in our whole neighborhood was that of the US Fifth Army. The main headquarters was up north in the old Chicago Beach Hotel and at Fort Sheridan, but there was another contingent in Hyde Park in a hotel just across from Jackson Park and the Museum of Science and Industry. They wore a unique red, white and blue patch with white "A-5" superimposed on a blue mosque. The significance of the mosque referred to the activation of that Army in 1943 in French Morocco.

General Mark Clark commanded the Fifth Army across North Africa and into Italy, where they attacked both the Italians and the Germans until the Italians quit and the Germans backed all the way up the boot from Sicily to Rome and beyond. They fought major battles at Anzio, Monte Cassino, the Rapido River, and the Winter Line, and suffered from the bitter weather and rugged terrain conditions. They saw 602 continuous days of combat! No weekends off and no summer vacations.

We didn't know all the details then. We looked at war as glamorous, wonderful and full of glory. We had no idea of what the awful reality was like. We played war games nonstop. We had no end of castoff army surplus stuff, helmets, old fatigues, toy rifles, entrenching tools, canteens, and packs of all kinds. We had some bitter battles with the neighboring Essex gang, who we equated with the Axis of Evil and attacked regularly with rocks, bows, and arrows made out of dried ragweed stalks, sticks, and clubs. Then we would head back to the safety of our own complex of forts and tree houses in our own prairie.

We saw movies and the newsreels which were all combat: Back to Bataan, They were Expendable, Flying Tigers, Sands of Iwo Jima, and my favorite, Battleground, about the Battle of the Bulge and the 101st Airborne Division at Bastogne. Talk about a brainwashed generation! I am surprised we didn't all join the military as fast as we could. Many of us did, of course, and served later in the Cold War. We were very lucky in hindsight. We came of age right in between the Korean War and Vietnam. Some of us were disappointed, but we were blessed and did not know it. I heard they even have a special new Cold War medal now. About time!

I remember scavenging in the alleys in the spring of '45 or '46 with Dick Coughlan and somebody else. We were always on the lookout for treasure and spring cleaning was a prime time. But we were not prepared for what we found behind one garage. There were boxes of German uniforms, a little moth-eaten but not too bad for wear. Standard kind of blue-green blouses and trousers. There were insignia and garrison caps and belts. This was a real haul and would be worth a lot today to a collector. We gathered all the boxes and made a beeline for our fort.

We played with the stuff, oversized as it was, and were having a great time until Mr. Coughlan came by and chewed us out. TJ and Dick's father had been a major in the military police attached to the prison at Pontiac about 100 miles south of Chicago and was in charge of German POWs. He was not at all happy about us playing with the stuff. "Boys," he said sternly, "You may think all this war stuff is a game! Well, I'm going to tell you that it is NOT a game and what you're doing is an insult to all of our brave soldiers who died or were wounded fighting against men wearing those uniforms you have on." We were in shock. What had we done wrong? We were just playing, for cripes sake!

"I want you boys to get those uniforms off right now. You can keep the insignia, but get the clothing off, pronto."

We did as ordered and took off as much of the insignia as we could with our pocket knives as Mr. Coughlan went into his garage and came back with a five gallon can of fuel oil. When we got all the uniforms together and made a pile in the prairie, he poured a generous amount of fuel over all of it and lit it with his lighter.

We were just stunned. The best stash we had ever found and now it was going up in smoke. It wasn't fair. But life isn't fair either. Except if you think about it, life isn't fair to anybody, so then doesn't that make it fair?

Anyway, we weren't ready yet for that kind of philosophizing. We just took the insignia we had left and split it up to stash in our cigar boxes at home. Tomorrow would be a better day.

And it was a better day. There was a Knights of Columbus "smoker" on 79th Street, featuring some fights between some of the up and coming Catholic Youth Organization boxers. There was no shortage of food with a grand buffet, open bar, and plenty of pop and snacks. It was a big deal for me and the few other boys who were allowed in. Male bonding, they call it now.

There was a boring business meeting to start out and I was glad to see Father Mac there. Father Mac (Ignatius McDermott to you) was a wonderful priest and a regular guy. He was a rebel though, and was always in some hot water with the big guy downtown, the Archbishop, who was the head of the whole Chicago Archdiocese.

Father Mac had been quite an athlete in his day and was interested in sports of all kinds. Even his car, after he became famous as the priest of Skid Row, had a sports-related license plate: #4. If you have to ask why #4, then you did not follow the White Sox very much or you would have known Luke Appling's number.

Part of the business meeting was to give awards to some of the guys there who had been in the war and been in the Bataan Death March in 1942 and survived it. Many of the Knights had been in the war, of course, and many of them were talking about where they had been and some of what they had seen. The more beer they drank, the louder they got and some of them were quite loud. One thing for sure, they did not like Bataan or the Japanese soldiers. After the awards were given to the three guys, Father Mac got up and talked, sort of like he did in church at Our Lady of Peace on Sundays.

Everybody was quiet now. All the folks in the neighborhood, whether Catholic or not, had great respect for Father McDermott. He was not pretentious. He was just a regular guy who talked to everybody, no matter how much money they had, where they lived or where they went to church. Father Mac talked about the terrible conditions these men had faced with the heat, lack of water, beatings, and guys getting their heads cut off or bayonetted to death. It was not easy to listen to and I looked over at the three men who had gotten the awards and they were looking grim. I looked around the hall and saw that other men had tears in their eyes. Very soon I did too and I looked up at my dad, who used to be a semipro baseball player before the war, and he had his hanky out dabbing at his eyes.

Nobody was drinking beer or eating now. The hall was dead silent. Even the servers and the CYO fighters were sitting and listening quietly. After Father Mac told about all the terrible sufferings of our soldiers, he told another story about the great baseball game.

Now, FatherMac was about as big a fan of the Chicago White Sox as there could be. A lot of his sermons revolved around sports and baseball and I think the movie Field of Dreams was his favorite movie of all time. But he was not talking about a movie. He was talking about a baseball game back on Bataan in 1942 at Camp O'Donnell after that brutal march of 70 miles without food or water in the heat and dust and being subjected to beatings, bayonetting and murder.

After a few weeks of men dying and being beaten severely, so many men were sick or gone that there were not enough living to bury the dead. After all that, the Japanese guards came to the GIs and told them they wanted to play a baseball game the next day. The Japanese had found sports equipment in one of the buildings and got the idea they would like to play the Americans and again show them the superiority of the Asians over the white men.

The American prisoners were stunned. They had trouble walking, let alone running the bases. They were starving and sick with dysentery and malaria and they were all nervous of what the soldiers might do during the game and then after, particularly if they lost. If the guards lost face in front of all of their comrades, the GIs felt there could be a bloodbath. The Americans had all seen the newsreels of the Japanese atrocities in Nanking.

Finally though, they had to select some volunteers and almost all the guys who could walk stepped forward to volunteer. With substitutes, the Americans had about twelve men who could barely take the field: nine players and a three man bench. Some of the players had played ball in high school and some even had college or semipro experience. They got together and looked into themselves to decide how they were going to play the situation. Play to win? Play to lose? Play not to win by very much? The question became how to handle the situation and not allow the Japanese guards to lose too much face.

I don't think the GIs slept too well that night. One thing was finally made clear. They decided to play to win, whatever the ultimate cost would be. "Screw it" one guy had said. "Let's kick their little yellow butts all the way back to Tokyo."

All they could do now is try to get some sleep. Some of the prisoners came over to the ballplayers with small food items that had been hidden away or picked up from prisoners who had died. "Go ahead and take it," they said quietly. "You're going to need all the strength you can get."

The game was set for ten in the morning after the guards had their morning exercises and then breakfast. The prisoners tried to do some basic stretching exercises and put on their best game faces. At least the game would be a break from the tedium and horror that was beginning to set in at the camp.

Around nine o'clock, two guards showed up in the barracks with mitts and a bat and a few old hardballs. One thing, the guards seemed to be in a fairly good mood. Maybe that was a positive sign. Maybe no beatings today—except on the field. The guys began to warm up and their morale began to rise.

Father Mac said that the Americans had a pretty good pitcher on the improvised mound. He had played semipro ball before the war and then enlisted before Pearl Harbor and had played for Schofield Barracks in Hawaii and done very well. The catcher was no slouch either so they had good strength up the middle. The American team met in a circle behind home plate. One of the guys growled quietly, "Look guys, whatever happens, let's give it everything we've got. We've had our butts kicked at Pearl and now at Corregidor and Bataan. We're not gonna let 'em whip us at our game. Let's kick their yellow butts!" The team cheered and the Japanese players, guards and spectators looked over quizzically.

The game was a back and forth affair for the first three innings or so. A low scoring, "small ball" game but the GIs were getting their wind back and getting into the game. They began slugging away, knocking one pitcher after another out of the ball game. The runs began to mount for the Americans and their spirits went up with the score. Even then they were careful not to show too much enthusiasm or do anything that would needlessly put all the prisoners in even more danger. The hits and runs just kept coming. Everything was going their way, and fairly soon the game was out of reach of the Japanese garrison. Finally, the last out was made and the Americans lined up along the third base line and bowed, expecting the worst. Amazingly, the guards did the same and then did the unbelievable: the guards went over to their dugout and gathered up handfuls of candy and cigarettes. They even broke out some cold rice beer and sake, and drinks were passed all around.

After that there was a definite change in the guards' behavior toward all the prisoners. Rations improved a bit and the beatings slacked off big-time. There was still a long way to go though, and many of the Americans still wound up on rust-bucket prison ships bound for the Japanese mainland and into slave labor. But they would carry with them for three long years and beyond the memory of that time they had defied death and kicked butt on Camp O'Donnell's baseball field.

When Father Mac finished there was not a dry eye in the hall. Even the fighters looked stunned. The awards were given out, the dinner finished, the cigarettes and cigars lit and the fights were on. Afterwards, as I wrote in a letter to my grandmother, "Father McDermott came up to me and punched me in the stomach!" It must have been my crowning moment, my "highlight reel" and it meant a lot to me because it meant I was just one of the guys.

My dad and I walked east back home along 79th Street, past the church and our local taverns, shops and stores and headed home. We could have taken the Red Rocket trolley car, but it was a cool night and we just wanted to walk and talk. At one point by Twin Liquors, I put my hand in his and asked, "Dad, why do wars and such bad things happen?"

"I don't know, son" he said pensively. "I don't know, but just remember that you have to be ready for all kinds of bad things, so just try to be the best that you can be in everything so you'll always be ready for the hard times, and pray for the strength to get through them and help others get through them as well."

I think I prayed all the way home and for some days after that. It was good to be safe in our little basement apartment, I remember that.

9

THE MAGICIAN IN THE GOLDEN CAGE

Living in Chicago during World War II did not allow us to see many German POWs, as most of the 644 POW camps were located in agricultural areas. The prisoners were taken to work on farms where they assisted in harvesting grain in the Dakotas, fruit in the Northwest, corn throughout the Midwest, and hemp in Iowa. Oddly enough, we did have some direct contact with them in South Shore between 1943 and 1945 through an unusual connection.

Our neighbors at 79th and Phillips were the Coughlans. They had two boys, T.J. and Dick. We were in constant conflicts as boys will be, in fights one minute and best buddies the next. Their dad, a Chicago lawyer in real life, became a Major in the U.S. Army and was assigned to downstate Pontiac prison south of Chicago. His job was to provide security for the flood of German prisoners that were coming to the U.S. at the request of the British, who, after the great victories in the Western Desert at El Alamein and Tobruk, simply did not have the manpower nor the resources to support them in Britain. So for these lucky battle-hardened veterans of Erwin Rommel's Afrika Korps, it was goodbye to Libya and hello to the Midwest. No Eastern front duty for these guys. They were now in what they called "der Goldener Kafig" or "The Golden Cage!"

Major Coghlan had good duty as far as assignments went in the service. He was close to home and could get back almost every weekend. The Coghlans were well off, and I remember that their grandmother lived at the South Shore Country Club at 71st and South Shore Drive, which was about the height of luxury as far as we knew it.

Negroes and Jews were excluded from membership then, but so were us "shanty Irish" and anybody else who couldn't pay the freight. In that sense it was a definite equal lack of opportunity situation. Didn't bother us any. The whole neighborhood and every "prairie" was our "Poor Boys" country club.

The Coghlans owned their own three story apartment building on 79th and Phillips, just a few buildings south of where we were renting a basement apartment at 7952. This kind of building required a great deal of maintenance and care, particularly in wartime with shortages of coal, manpower, and supplies.

Major Coghlan had a secret weapon. Every weekend it seemed there was an endless parade of German POWs from Pontiac prison who would make the trip up to our South Shore neighborhood to mow the lawn, shovel coal, wash windows and do repairs and painting around the place, and I suppose around some other apartment buildings in our area. If you think about it, why should the farmers have been the only recipients of free labor? After all, city kids were fighting on all fronts, just like the farm boys.

So they came. A regular stream of Hanses, Wolfs, Dieters, Manfreds and Sepps arrived with the Major in an olive drab U.S. Army Jeep on Friday afternoons, and stayed for the weekend. They looked like ordinary guys to us, no supermen here. They were quiet but cheerful for the most part, even joking around with us kids from time to time, but always somewhat careful and reserved like someone who knows he has a winning lottery ticket and doesn't want to jinx himself in any way. He watches the traffic signs and crosses the street a little more carefully.

For the most part we accepted them as normal. They looked about like anyone else in Chicago and many of us had German ancestors in our backgrounds, mine coming to Wisconsin about a century before, just in time for the Civil War. Welcome to the Union, Johann!

I do not remember them wearing anything that marked them as POWs. Overalls, dungarees and common work clothing were nothing new. They could have fit in anywhere in any working class neighborhood in Chicago, particularly on the south side and as close to the steel mills as we were.

Our contacts with them were sporadic and they did not seem different from anyone else of that age, which was anyone over the age of 15. People that old were in another category anyway, since we were just five and six or seven at the time. Strangely enough, we did not bedevil them in any way, and I do not remember that there was any sense of fear on our part. They were simply old guys, even if some of them were only ten years or so older than us.

They did not seem to be under any kind of guard particularly, and that, as much as anything, probably helped us to accept them. Ironically, they helped out in our local victory gardens in the prairies between Yates Boulevard and Phillips, which were located along the railroad that ran daily coal cars to the steel mills in South Chicago. I think they enjoyed the gardening and the camaraderie of the neighborhood.

Even in the early- to mid-1940s, with evidence of the war all around us, we were not yet touched by the propaganda. These particular men who had been in a vast and savage desert war were somehow different and less marked than those who were involved later in the death camps or who had committed atrocities in Poland, the Soviet Union or at places like Malmedy.

It was odd that we were never warned to avoid them. I don't remember being told to stay away from them or being told that they were in any way bad or harmful. We would see them from time to time even up at the Porcelain Palace, the White Castle on the corner of 79th and Essex Avenue. The ironic thing was, it was right in the middle of one of the most Jewish of all Chicago neighborhoods. At the time we didn't, and I'm sure the adults didn't, have any inkling about the real German policy toward the Jews and others who didn't fit into the master plan for the Third Reich.

I can remember a couple of them being present and watching silently as a U.S. Marine Corps drill team from Great Lakes Naval Training Center assisted in the dedication of the little park located on Phillips a half block south of us. I was sick and could not go out, but they drifted over when the entire Marine drill team came to my basement window to say, hello and get well at the request of my dad.

One English-speaking POW in particular I remember as being extremely kindly, engaging and cheerful. He was a whiz at doing all kinds of magic tricks. Most were the adroit sleight of hand that made coins appear from behind our ears or seeing a small toy disappear, only to reappear in his shirt pocket. We were not only a good audience, but at our age, four to seven, we must have been a poignant reminder of German children back home in Pomerania, Stuttgart, or even Berlin.

One particular delight, and I don't know how he did it to this day, was to somehow roll up an old Trib or Daily News after showing us that there was nothing inside the pages. He waved a slender, colorful carved magic wand that appeared out of nowhere and after a suitable amount of time and incantations he would hand the newspaper back to us. We would open it excitedly, unrolling the pages which were now filled with what seemed to be hundreds of colorful coupons. We were informed that these were magic gilders, and we were mightily impressed.

We would gather them up and save them to cash in for candy up at Alpert's grocery on 79th St. To our chagrin, we were duly informed by old man Alpert that, while they might well be magic gilders, they were still not legal tender in the U.S. It was not until a few years later when we could read and "Der Magician" had long since disappeared, that we found out the magic gilders were in fact just Ivory soap coupons. No matter. They were our gilders and they became magic to us. Maybe enemies are human after all.

10

1947: REMEMBER THE TARS (AND DON'T FORGET THE BIG RED AND THE IRISH)

Sports in old South Shore were like a second religion to us Catholic kids. We worshipped Notre Dame, the University of Illinois, the Chicago White Sox, and the Chicago Cardinals. At the high school level in the Catholic League we followed Mount Carmel, Leo, St. Rita, and DeLaSalle on the South side. In the Public League we kept a close eye on the big south-siders like Chicago Vocational School, Lindblom, Fenger and Calumet. Most of all, we cheered our own 1947 South Shore High School football team.

1947 was a banner sports year in the Chicago area. Notre Dame went unbeaten and untied to a national championship with our own Ziggie Czarobski and George Connor. The Chicago Cardinals finally got to the top of the NFL with the dream backfield of Paul Christman, Elmer Angsman, Pat Harder and Charlie Trippi, along with Marshall Goldberg and our own Chet

Bulger, who coached and mentored many of us at De-LaSalle in later years.

The most important team locally was our own South Shore Tars, whose colors were blue and green for Lake Michigan and whose mascots were the British seamen of the Royal Navy. Not that we were pretentious or anything, but South Shore had some strong British connections in its early days with Welsh, English and Irish laborers working on the Illinois Central railroad and the construction boom south of Jackson Park during and after the Columbian Exposition of 1893. Because of them, we had areas known as Bryn Mawr, Chatham, Windsor and Windsor Park, Cheltenham, and even a lawn bowling club in Jackson Park.

South Shore High School was still fairly new, with construction completed in the early 1940s. The school took in Bowen High School's population from South Chicago one class year at a time. I have a photograph taken in 1939 when I was a year old, being held by my dad standing next to his father.

1947: REMEMBER THE TARS

My Grandpa Lewis had arrived in Chicago at age ten from England with his parents just in time for the 1893 World's Fair in newly developed Jackson Park between South Shore and Hyde Park.

The Tars were never known for their football prowess, although they once boasted Marv Levy, of Buffalo Bills fame, as a star running back. They were more likely to excel at basketball, baseball, golf, bowling, or tennis. However, the 1947 football season was one for the ages. This was a real Cinderella team. They literally came out of nowhere onto the Public League scene. They could only field a team of thirteen guys total. Eleven went both ways almost all season, with a bench of two other stalwarts. I don't even know if that would be allowed today.

I remember my dad taking me into the South Shore locker room after one of the 1947 season games, probably to see a couple of our neighbor kids who were on that team. They must have won the game because the showers seemed full of exuberant and naked young athletes with an abundance of youthful energy and enthusiasm. They were just ecstatic, laughing and snapping towels at each other; shouting and singing, the walls just echoing with all the pride and optimism only the young can muster up. It was a wonderful moment and within ten years I would be in the same locker room and in the same showers, with a different team, but no less rowdy and enthusiastic.

They did not even have regular game uniforms, as I was told by my folks later, and had to borrow practice uniforms from nearby Hirsch High School to play their games. I remember that they did have their own blue and green helmets: the Riddell suspension, or bucket helmets, that were much in vogue at the time. There were no face masks, of course.

The band and the ROTC marching corps of cadets outnumbered the football players by almost six to one. That says a lot about the importance and value of the football program in the Public League. Maybe it was the University of Chicago's de-emphasis of intercollegiate football in 1939 that caused it, I don't know. I just know that was not the case with the Catholic League in Chicago, which went all out for athletics then and now. Leo, Mount Carmel and St. Rita were the class of the south side while Weber, Fenwick and St. George were the toast of the north side.

The Chicago Public League always seemed to be scraping to get everything from new uniforms, helmets, good coaches, and real support. Not that the Public League did not have their own powerhouses. Schools like Austin, CVS, Schurz, Fenger and Lane Tech were no slouches in anybody's book.

The Catholic League schools could recruit from anywhere, even outside the city, and they had alumni and parent support groups that funded new equipment and uniforms. For them, it was nothing but the best. Rumor had it that the football backers group, or just some renegade alumni at Mount Carmel, bought their star running back of the early 1950s a new convertible, among other things.

My future high school, DeLaSalle, even had its own "over the road" bus (a retired Greyhound) and our football summer camp was a two week, "two a day" deal up in Wisconsin near Eagle River. For many of us, it was the first time we were ever outside Chicago, certainly outside Illinois.

1947 was the year that really cemented my interest in football. We lived at 7952 S. Phillips Avenue, and just a couple of blocks south was the Chicago Park District's Eckersall Stadium. It was a first class high school stadium, used by many local schools, including South Shore and Mount Carmel. The challenge for my buddies and me was always to get in without paying. We would go over the fence when we could, under when we had to, hand out programs or make ourselves useful but never, never fork over any dough except for popcorn and other treats.

We saw many great football games at Eckersall, named for old Walter Eckersall, who was all of 5 feet 7 inches tall and weighed in at 142 pounds. In the early 1900s, Walter was the real deal. He could do it all and had plenty of speed and talent to run, punt and drop kick. He went to Hyde Park High School up by Jackson Park, which oddly enough, was the site of Buffalo Bill's Wild West show during the Columbian Exposition's World Fair in 1893. From there he went to the University of Chicago and became one of Walter Camp's first All-Americans around 1910.

Mount Carmel was the absolute powerhouse of the late '40s and early '50s, but South Shore came up with its own legend in 1947. They were anchored by Tommy O'Connell, halfback; Pete Bachourous, running back; Rex Smith, tight end; and Dan Sabino at center. Obviously, the whole team played both ways with only two subs on the sidelines. Tommy O'Connell was drafted by the Cleveland Browns in the 1952 NFL draft. He eventually took over the legendary Otto Graham's place and later was traded to the Chicago Bears.

This exceptional South Shore team took their league championship and wound up playing the west side Austin Tigers, a perennially strong team that produced Abe Woodson, who went on to the University of Illinois and to an NFL career. The Public League championship game was played at Soldier Field on November 23, 1947.

The game was tied at halftime 0-0, to give an idea of how well matched these two teams were. In the early minutes of the fourth quarter, with South Shore trailing 7-6, Tommy O'Connell dropped back to throw a pass to end Ray Lawlor near the end zone. The ball was intercepted and run back by Austin, who eventually scored twice and sealed the fate of the Tars, who simply ran out of gas at the end. For the Tars, the clock struck midnight and the beautiful coach turned into a pumpkin for our Cinderella.

Austin went on the next week to play Leo, the Catholic league champs for the Kelly Bowl City championship, again at Soldier Field, and defeated Leo by a one point margin: 13-12. If the Tars had had some reserve strength, what a different story it all could have been. It was not over for four young men on the South Shore team. They would get another day of real glory as University of Illinois football players when they dismantled Stanford 40-7 in the 1952 Rose Bowl. I don't know, but I'm willing to bet that the Fighting Illini had more than two players on the sidelines in Pasadena on that January day.

If you lived on Chicago's south side when we were kids, say in the 1940s and 1950s, right up to 1960 when everything seemed to change, your allegiances to pro sports were very simple. You and your family and your friends for the most part were White Sox baseball fans, Chicago Cardinals football fans, and both sides of town enjoyed the Blackhawks hockey team. The Bulls were not yet in existence as far as basketball and your favorite college team for anything was Notre Dame if you were Catholic and if you were Irish and_Catholic there was no doubt: you worshipped at the Golden Dome in South Bend even if you had never been further east of Chicago than Phil Smidt's restaurant on Indianapolis Boulevard.

The real rivalry in pro sports in the Windy City was between the Chicago Bears on the north side and the Chicago Cardinals on the south. George Halas, the Bears owner, hated the Cards with a passion only he could muster up. He lived for the day when he could see his red and white archrivals driven out of town. He finally got his wish in 1960 when the Cards moved to St. Louis, home of those other famous redbird teams.

The Cardinals remain today in Arizona as the oldest continuously run football team in the United States. They built strong teams in the 1920s, 1940s, and the 1970s, capturing two NFL titles and four division crowns during those decades. The greatest of them all by acclaim were our heroes, the 1947 champions of the old south side with their million dollar backfield of quarterback Paul Christman, fullback Pat Harder from Wisconsin and halfbacks Elmer Angsman (from Mount Carmel High School) and Charley Trippi.

Not long before, in the war year of 1944, with the manpower-depleted NFL, the Cards were merged with the Pittsburgh Steelers to form the forgettable "Card-Pitts" otherwise known as the Carpets because "everyone walked all over them."

From 1946 to 1948, head coach Jimmy Conzelman led the Cardinals to three consecutive winning seasons. Their dream backfield had overwhelming offensive production for the time and they rolled through the '47 season, finally defeating the Philadelphia Eagles 28-21 before a crowd of 30,759 in old Comiskey Park in a "thrilling game marked by long runs," as David Condon wrote. All four Cardinal touchdowns were accounted for by Charley Trippi and Elmer Angsman. The rest was history.

I was fortunate to be present when that team finally got their championship rings. In 1997, after years of Bidwell family thrift, the rings were finally handed out to the remaining players. Better late than never, I guess.

We stayed connected to the Cards through loyalty and the mentorship of Mr. Chet Bulger, coach and teacher at DeLaSalle High School. Chet was star left tackle on that championship team and spent ten years in the NFL, eventually retiring from the Detroit Lions with an NFL pension of some $40 a month. He, and many others, played in the pre-1960 big TV money contracts and were forgotten by the league and the later players.

Chet coached at St. Mary's College in Winona, Minnesota with the Christian brothers and then came to DeLaSalle in the late 1950s after St. Mary's dropped football. He made millions in good will but not much cash. In 2008 Coach Chet Bulger was honored with the dedication of the new DeLaSalle stadium in his name at 35th and Wabash next to the El tracks and almost in the shadow of the new White Sox ball park. It could not have happened to a nicer guy!

The "Fighting Irish" football teams need no introduction to most sport fans around the country. For at least four decades they dominated college football like few other teams and won the hearts of fans that would never ever see the beautiful campus in South Bend, Indiana, let alone attend school there.

The mid '40s (especially '44 and '45) were dominated by the great Army teams of Earl "Red" Blaik and stars like Glen Davis and Felix "Doc" Blanchard. On the side of Rockne Gymnasium at Notre Dame, emblazoned in stone, is the crest of the U.S. Military Academy at West Point. What greater respect could be paid to an arch rival of the great teams of the 40s from both schools? After the war, the tide shifted back to the civilian schools and Notre Dame dominated above all others. Notre Dame won the national championship in 1946, while the 1947 Notre Dame football squad remains one of the greatest teams ever assembled by a school known for outstanding football teams. Led by Coach Frank Leahy and captained by DeLaSalle's own George Connor, this team was one for the ages. Sports Illustrated and a number of other national publications later called the 1947 team "the greatest football team ever assembled." Notre Dame as a whole enjoyed a four year run not likely to be bettered: three national championships and one other undefeated season for a four year run without a single loss.

The '47 backfield of Emil Sitko, John Panelli, Terry Brennan and Johnny Lujack was one of Notre Dame's best of all time. Our own Ziggy Czarobski from South Chicago and Leon Hart, as well as George Connor, anchored a line that was totally dominant for that unbelievable four-year stretch.

We listened to the radio broadcasts on Saturday afternoons, dreaming of a time that we would be able to play for the Irish at Notre Dame. Connor and Lujack went on to the Chicago Bears, Hart to the Detroit Lions, Panelli eventually to the Cards and Ziggy Czarobski to his own restaurant on South 83rd Street near the old neighborhood.

I have to admit to some ambivalent feelings about Notre Dame. I suppose some of that comes from the fact that going to school there was not in the cards, athletically, academically, or financially. I wish that I could have gone there in so many ways. Later in life, I did get to Notre Dame for a number of visits and saw an interesting side to the Notre Dame experience. I was so impressed that student life revolves entirely around the dormitory. A student is in the same dorm for all four years and this means student government as well as extracurricular activities were tied to the dorm. In addition, varsity athletes are assigned to all dorms. There is no single "jock" dorm, like so many big powerhouses. Attachment at the school has to be very powerful indeed. Your dorm mates become your other family and the bonding there has to be a great part of the entire Notre Dame experience.

My insurance agent in Chicago was Tom Weir, who was a Notre Dame grad and was Rocky Bliers' roommate at Notre Dame for four years, including the golden year of the 1966 national champs. Tom talked me into playing rugby football in Chicago for the Lincoln Park Rugby team, a team that will go down in rugby history for its diversity if nothing else. What a mix. Doctors and med students, lawyers and law students, educators, advertising execs and businessmen side by side with unemployed actors, professional puppeteers, and long haired loonies of all kinds. We had Blacks, Jews, Irish Catholics, Protestants, whatever and whoever answered the call each season in Chicago.

Well, Tom talked Rocky into playing one season with us to get him back into football shape since he was drafted by the Pittsburgh Steelers before going to Vietnam. There he was seriously wounded and almost lost his foot. Rocky gave us a real boost that season. He went on to the Steelers' training camp the following summer and the rest, as they say, was history. He was a steady, reliable and durable running back in the Terry Bradshaw, Lynn Swann, John Stallworth, Jack Lambert and Franco Harris era. The group won four Super Bowl rings in all and a place in sports history that will be remembered for a long time to come. That was as close as I ever got to playing with a real "domer." Go Irish!

11

THE SHERMAN SAGA: THE SHERMANS OF SOUTH SHORE

All families have themes. Sometimes those themes are wonderfully harmonious in nature with a cohesiveness that transcends generations, binding years of ups and downs, struggles, joys, illnesses, travels, sorrows and all the other parts of our social DNA together in a series of movements and fugues like a great symphony playing in concert with the cosmos of our lives. Those mystic chords of memory and the ongoing sense of family are what really binds us today.

The Shermans of South Shore had a multitude of positive themes that made them stand out in a very special neighborhood in ways that paralleled not only our immigrant experience but the development of our country and the city of Chicago, down to the present day and beyond.

The Sherman home up the street from us was always a delight for me to visit. It was a real haven and comfort for me in troubled times. I felt a welcoming sense of warmth and family from all the Shermans, or at least as many as there were in the late '40s and early '50s. Because, as I found out later, dad Orville and mom Elinore Sherman had the foresight to add Kathleen and Nancy to provide some needed balance to the three boys I grew up with: Jim, Danny, and Terry.

Their two flat at 7630 Constance, directly across from South Shore High School, was always a popular gathering place for kids from the neighborhood, including the Porter girls, John Onufrock, Mark Carpenter, Art Drea, Johnny Florsheim, the Sheehans, Jack and Bobby, Dave Dillon, Oakie Dowling and Jerry Levine. They all added variety and interest to those growing up years. The closeness of the neighborhood is evident by the way Jim still talks about the neighbors as if they were still there. Other neighbors included the Browns, John and Nita and their girls, the Onufrocks, Buschbaums, Barb and Jackie, the Strausers, and Obshers, as well as Old Dr. Wall, who was the Shermans' (and half the neighborhood's) family doctor along with the Wall kids: Josie, Pete, Bob, Jack, Jim, and I don't know who all else might have been added to that family as well.

We moved to 7711 Constance in 1949, into my maternal grandparents Joe and Rowena Hannan's first floor two flat. Great Uncle Ed Hannan and his wife Amy continued to live upstairs where they had lived since 1926 and my dad's father, Albert Lewis, had moved into an apartment at 7735 Constance in 1935. I was not a stranger to Constance nor to South Shore, having been raised there off and on all my early days.

For some odd reason, I have always connected the Sherman house with the Crusades. Perhaps it was because as children we were so closely involved with and influenced by the greatest crusade of our time: World

War II. The Shermans had tons of books and some of the most interesting and unique furniture around, although that fit another of their themes, the furniture moving business.

The old, musty, oversized books on the Crusades really made an impression on a young boy in the days before television. The books were full of black and white lithographs (remember, the world was in black and white in those days!) of the lionhearted King Richard doing bloody battle with the Saracens of Saladin. Pictures showed stormed castles, burning torsos, impaled warriors, headless bodies and bodiless heads by the thousands. There were flags, banners, shields and an ocean of spear points glistening in the desert as far as the eye could see!

Gustave Dore's apocalyptic drawings gripped our imaginations and held us in a magic sway that was more powerful than all the celluloid magic of the Avalon, the Jeffery and even the Chelten theater with its weekly episodes of The Mummy with Lon Chaney. We read the books and absorbed the pictures while sitting enthroned on Arthurian furniture, wonderfully carved gothic pieces that only added to the Colleen Moore dollhouse atmosphere.

But we were not a passive lot. Quickly we translated our active imaginations into a host of homemade weapons: bows and arrows, slingshots, rocks and ragweed spears while doing fierce battle on the nearby prairies of the South Shore neighborhood against ourselves and all enemies, foreign and domestic, with an intensity that would have pleased Pope Urban II and Emperor Fredrick Barbarossa.

We graduated in June of 1952 from Our Lady of Peace, that great Romanesque structure with the dollar green doors at 79th and Jeffery. Jim Sherman went on to

Leo High School. This was an aberration as most of our OLP classmates went directly to Mount Carmel. There at Leo, with the Irish Christian Brothers (who kept the other Christian Brothers in the wine business) Jim ran track. He was always a naturally good athlete, particularly at sandlot baseball on prairies with baseballs that were wrapped in electrical tape that became heavy as a rock over time. A darn good boxer he was too, making up for lack of size with lightning moves, quickness, agility and most of all the intelligence to stay out of the almost constant and senseless brawling going on around us.

We all had our share of what are now called entry level jobs. "Slave labor" would have been a little more accurate. So work we did. Small jobs mainly, shoveling snow, delivering papers, cutting lawns, caddying at Jackson Park and South Shore Country Club. Later we would graduate to delivering groceries and pizza.

Jim worked for the Windsor Park News Agency (Windsor Park being the last vestige of the British railway workers who had come to South Shore in the late 1880s to work on the original Illinois Central commuter station at 71st and Jeffery Boulevard) while Phil Jordan and I labored for 'Greasy Al' Liss at the South Chicago Agency. Jim later had a job working all through high school at Wee Folks toy store for Manny and Belle Lazar.

Somehow, Jim got into the Sea Scouts out of Jackson Park Harbor when the rest of us were trying to make it in the Boy Scouts. The Sea Scouts definitely had more class. They had real lifeboats like the Aussies on Bondi Beach. This may have been where Jim learned the value of teamwork—everyone pulling together for a common cause. The metaphors are appropriate: they provided a safe harbor for him and they showed him the right way like a lighthouse. Most importantly, they showed him the value of knowing what to do when you're up a creek without a paddle!

In grade school, and I suspect in high school as well, as later at St. Xavier and Loyola, Jim was the class of the class. He and classmate Terry Tobin were intellectually above the rest of us. However, unlike many others who are gifted, Jim never lost that common touch. He was always close with those of us who labored in the back of the room. He never became arrogant as many gifted kids are. It was a good thing too because as all talented folks eventually find out is that even though they are eagles, they will have to work with a host of turkeys in their lifetime!

My family came apart at the seams in 1952 during my first year at South Shore High School and we five children were scattered from Angel Guardian Orphanage to Roseland, and to my grandparents' home in Cedar Lake, Indiana. I had the good fortune to be accepted at Our Lady of the Ozarks Oblate Seminary the next year and went down to Carthage, Missouri with a large group of other Our Lady of Peace classmates, giving me the most stable and successful year in my youth. My parents reunited the next year and I was able to come home. The problem was that they had moved north to 67th and Blackstone in Woodlawn and I enrolled at DeLaSalle Institute, effectively taking me both out of the old neighborhood in South Shore and into the teeth of the storms of racial change.

In my mind, the watershed year in our lives was 1960. Before that, life existed as whole different glorious time of innocence, youth, dances and Friday night socials, ball games, fun, lazy summer days at Rainbow Beach – the forties and fifties were a special time for all of us in Chicago no matter what neighborhood or parish we were from. Our new families and our own children became the priority for us and we learned to grow up. We learned how to change from being parented, to being a parent, to caring for our own parents as they aged. After 1960 it seemed that something vital collapsed and nothing was ever quite the same again: So long to old South Shore.

Goodbye to Ike and to Mamie. Enter the Beatles, drugs, and Vietnam. Goodbye to JFK, then RFK. Goodbye to Martin Luther King. Hello to riots, looting, burning, and LBJ. Hello to Vatican II and guitar masses. Goodbye to our old Latin liturgy. Howdy to Tricky Dick Nixon and so long to Adlai Stevenson and Estes Kefauver and Hubert Humphrey. Goodbye to 58,000 of our youngest and most vulnerable young people in Vietnam as the Everly Brothers song went: "Goodbye happiness, hello loneliness: I think I'm gonna die." Hello adulthood, goodbye sports. Hello bills, debts, and mortgages. Hello new Wee Folks: children, toys, and diapers.

Goodbye Molines I and II; Hello McDonalds. Hellow METRA; goodbye old IC. Goodbye Avalon, Chelten and Jeffery theaters; hello New Regal Theater. Goodbye old Red Rockets trolley cars, hello to new green buses and hello to violence and chaos. Goodbye to Manny Lazar. Hello Blackstone Rangers and Black Panthers too; Goodbye old Southmoor Hotel.

Goodbye to our old South Shore Country Club; Hello South Shore Cultural Center. Goodbye Kickapoo Inn, Miner-Dunn, Cunises and Mitchells. Goodbye to Old Green River and Hello to Mountain Dew. So long Pla-Mor and Tastee-Freeze; "Hello emptiness; I think I'm gonna cry."

Goodbye to Twin Liquors, the Red Keg, the Emerald Isle. The Top Hat, the Brown Derby and service with a smile. Goodbye to Harkie's Barrel Pub at 2222 E. 79th St. So long to our good nuns, we hate to see you go, we really do. Hello to high school; hello to college and law school. Goodbye to weddings, hello to funerals, Goodbye to Mary Ann and Suzanne and our six other student nurses, may God bless you all.

Adios to Loretto, Aquinas, OLP, St. Brides, and St. Phillip Neri. Hello to the south suburbs, St. Agnes, Infant Jesus of Prague, St Lawrence O'Toole, St. Josephs and St. Michaels too. Goodbye to Anastasia, Kathleen, Marilyn, Josie and Lois. Hello to Marcia, Patricia, Peggy and Barbara.

Goodbye to play and hello to work. On the bright side, we still had LaFrance Laundry! Thank you, Mike and Tom Barth.

Enter Barbara: Stage Left

> "I am a Catholic Girl...
>
> My kisses are worth more than a hamburger, a car ride or a movie.
> My body is the temple of God-not a plaything.
> The first "NO" may be difficult-after that it's easy.
> Virginity is still a virtue, lust still a capital sin.
> The way I dress, act, and speak may be a temptation to my boyfriend.
> I will observe modesty for his and my own protection.
> My parents have done so much for me I wish always to be a credit to them.
> I will do nothing on my dates that I would be ashamed to tell them.
> My boyfriend will be a husband and father someday.
> He must be a hero in the eyes of his wife and children.
> I will do nothing to prevent that on
> my dates with him.

I want to be a wife and mother.
I will reserve my purity and affection for my husband and children.
Mary is my Mother, my Example, my ideal."

- St. Laurence Parish Bulletin, January 31, 1960

Jim Sherman and his beautiful bride, Miss Barbara Lauterbach had the good fortune to meet while sophomores in high school. The young couple never looked back. High school sweethearts from Leo and Loretto Englewood, they would be married in 1959. Of all of our OLP class of 1952, Jim and Barbara hold the record for the first wedding and for the longest (consecutive) marriage.

To me, Barbara represents all the best in American/Chicago/Catholic motherhood. Serene, stable, warm, bright, giving and generous to a fault, she and Jim have had a marvelous marriage. Like most marriages along the way, the kids started coming. Melissa (Brown) came along in 1960. Next came Jacqueline in '61 and James Wilson Jr. in '63. Next was Christina Berge in '65, Matthew in '66, and then in a grand finale: David and Andrew in '69.

Jim graduated from Chicago Loyola in 1963, the year Loyola took the NCAA championship. He went on and graduated with a Master's degree from St. Xavier in 1971. He had a varied and interesting career. He began with the Illinois Department of Corrections from 1973 to 1977 as Director of Legislation and Community Affairs.

Like his dad, Orville, who was a WPA actor, Jim maintains a strong love and allegiance to the theater. Always active in this field, perhaps it should have been his career, especially with that booming radio voice that he inherited from his Uncle Val Sherman (Remember the old "HUDSON TWO-THREE SEVEN HUNDRRRRED!" for Boushelle Rug Cleaners?).

From 1977 to 1982, Jim really got into politics. Grandpa Joe would have been proud. In 1982 Jim went to work for old Ben Bohac's LaSalle Talman Bank. Bought out by a Dutch firm without a clue as to the word "loyalty," the bottom line resulted in the now classic word in our vocabulary: Corporate downsizing. They also call it rightsizing. I say it's more like "wrongsizing" but then you know the new golden rule: "Do it to others before they do it to you."

COMING TO AMERICA

The migration to America begins with Jim's grandfather Joseph, who came to this country from the Sturm and Drang of the disputed territory of Alsace and Lorraine. Fought over through the centuries, the area was hard hit during the Franco-Prussian war of 1870. For a number of reasons, Grandfather Joseph Sherman (originally Josef Schermann) decided to vacate Europe. America was booming with new growth and transcontinental development. The old country ways were rigid and stifling: "you will be a baker, just like your father!" Substitute clerk, farmer, mechanic, or postman, and you get the picture. Coupled with the ongoing threat of conscription and endless warfare, many German families made the decision to come to the New World.

The struggles with new customs, finances, drought, extremes of weather, languages, sickness, and job searching had to take their toll. Joseph Sherman originally settled into the Molly Maguire coal and steel area but did not stay long. Joseph had the uncanny good fortune to find in Pennsylvania an Irish bride and frontier teacher named Mamie Doherty. Moving and transportation thereby came early to the family themes. Joseph Sherman apparently saw an opportunity out west. He apprenticed as a law clerk in the same way Abe Lincoln had done a generation before in New Salem, Illinois. The Shermans, like others of the time, tried a variety of things to keep afloat out on the Dakota plains, eventually settling in Belle Forche. Grandfather Sherman read law as he worked in the U.S. government land office in Belle. He and Mamie also ran a restaurant called the Sherman Family Beanery and Bakery. The restaurant boasted good food and rooms to let upstairs. (Respectable folks only!)

The story is still recalled in Chicago that settlers were escorted at one point from Belle to Fort Pierre, now the capital, for their safety during the last of the many Sioux Indian uprisings and reprisals for treaty violations in the Black Hills area. One of the common signs of the times in Belle that the Shermans no doubt saw was: "Head of a Sioux—$5.00."

In the middle of one of the richest grain belts in the world, the Shermans never farmed. They were always working townspeople but still struggled with unpredictable weather, predictable debt, and unpredictable people. Grandfather Sherman's struggles, including a run for the U.S. Congress in 1916 as a Wilson Democrat in a Rupublican era, led to a nervous breakdown and he eventually died in an institution in Fort Dodge, Iowa.

Jim's dad, Orville, was a second to the last of seven children, children being another recurring theme in the Sherman saga. Jim's two oldest uncles were both dentists who were sent to Chicago for school in the 1920s. They settled into South Woodlawn in the St.

Laurence Parish. In time the others all returned to the Midwest.

The following passage from Willa Cather's O, Pioneers! illustrates how fine the margin is between success and failure on the great plains:

> "For the first three years after John Bergson's death, the affairs of his family prospered. Then came the hard times that brought every one on the divide to the brink of despair; three years of drought and failure, the last struggle of a wild soil against the encroaching plowshare. The failure of the corn crop made labor cheap. Lou and Oscar hired two men and put in bigger crops than ever before. They lost everything they spent. The whole country was discouraged. Farmers who were already in debt had to give up their land. A few foreclosures demoralized the country. The settlers sat about on the wooden sidewalks in the little town and told each other that the country was never meant for men to live in; the thing to do was to get back to Iowa, to Illinois, to any place that had been proved habitable. The Bergson boys would have been happier with their Uncle Otto in the bakery shop in Chicago. Like most of their neighbors, they were meant to follow in the paths already marked out for them, not to break trails in a new country."
>
> - Willa Cather's O, Pioneers!

AN AMERICAN FAMILY

Jim's mother's (Elinore Pierce's) family roots go even deeper into the fabric of this country. Her great-grandfather Collin came over with Lafayette during the American Revolution. The Pierces had produced Franklin Pierce, (1804-1869) the 14th president of the United States, whose father Benjamin had also served in the Revolutionary Army.

Franklin Pierce was promoted to the rank of general and served under Winfield Scott on the U.S. Army expedition to Mexico City and the Halls of Montezuma in 1847, later becoming president in 1852 during the ominous and dark years before the Civil War. Exactly one hundred years later, both Jim and I would be working at the two great political conventions in Chicago 1952. Thus the Sherman family roots are about as classic as you could get on the south side of Chicago by the middle of the 20th century.

The Collin and Pierce families represented to a degree the "old money" and aristocracy such as it was in a new country. Moving west to Chicago, they too came to South Shore in the first quarter century.

South Shore was in a speculation boom period in the roaring twenties, with apartment buildings and businesses going up from the lake to Stony Island and from the steel mills to Jackson Park. My grandfather Joe Hannan had an electrical shop at 67th and Stony, not but a few doors away from Peggy's grandfather Percy Lynn's plumbing business. An apartment building could be put up for $10,000 and sold as every floor went higher for another $10,000. Speculation was rampant and everyone was anxious to make a killing.

Then came the depression. The lights went out all over Chicago and the businesses soon went with them. We would not come out of it until Franklin Roosevelt's New Deal and World War II.

THE SOUNDS OF MUSIC

Another recurring theme from the Shermans was that of music. Jim's mom Elinor was trained as a concert pianist under that famous Chicago martinet and legend, Rudolph Ganz, at the Chicago Conservatory of Music. Now part of Roosevelt University's School of Music and very closely allied with the Chicago Symphony Orchestra, the Chicago Conservatory was and in a sense still is a valuable piece of Chicago history.

Jim remembers his grandmother taking him, at age seven, for an audition with legendary Father O'Malley of the famous Paulist Boys Choir at Old St. Mary's Church at 11th and Wabash in the South Shore Loop area. Jim would travel from South Shore to St. Mary's via the Illinois Central from 71st and Jeffery and back alone. That in itself tells more about what the old days and values were than anything else could do.

Music was always in the air at 7630 Constance. The priests from Our Lady of Peace would come over on a regular basis: Fathers Thomas Bryne and Ignatius McDermott would come over away from the ever watchful eye of Monsignor Friel, and loosen their collars a bit, if not take them off altogether, and relax with Orville, the old actor turned transportation expert, enjoying a cold bottle of Meister Brau while singing along with Elinore at the piano. Sister Kathleen now carries on this family tradition as the Singing Nun, producing a host of albums for children. Jim's next younger brother Dan also found a career in music. After graduation from Leo High School and Quincy College, Dan, like Mr. Holland of Mr. Holland's Opus, settled down for a long run as a music director for the Quincy, Illinois public schools.

HERNIATED MOVERS AND WWII

Orville Sherman was not around home as much, being as busy and involved in the moving business as he was. Moving, both themselves and others, was another powerful theme in the Sherman saga. Maternal Grandfather Wilson Collin forged the deal with Martin Kennelly that brought together Allied Van Lines and eventually began Empire Movers, where Orville would spend his career.

Youngest brother Terry Sherman is in the same business today and living out in the western suburb of Wheaton. The business have gone from great moves across seas in leaky weather-beaten ships to covered wagons, grueling train rides cross-continent all the way to the big eighteen wheelers of Allied Van lines and Empire movers. Paul Newman said Bette Davis told him one time, "Gettin' old ain't for sissies!" Well, Paul, I got news for you: the moving business can be brutal and it ain't for sissies either.

Pianos and refrigerators were carried up three story buildings all over Hyde Park and South Shore. Working long hours in broiling Chicago summers and freezing winters with the winds howling down across Canada and down the Great Lakes was a tough way to make a buck. There were smashed fingers, twisted backs and hernias. You haven't been there unless you've humped a reefer down from a three flat alone with only a hempen cord twisted around your shoulders. The Irish movers always seemed to be doing penance, although what the excuse was for the Germans and Dutch, I don't know. Maybe that was why Orville Sherman, like his father before him, always pushed the kids into schooling. He could see the writing on the wall: very soon the day would no longer be there when a young south side kid could leave high school, get a job in a local factory or moving firm, or even with the city, and retire forty-odd years later with a modest pension and a cheap watch.

During the war years, Orville hit every enlistment office of every branch of service. He was turned down because of his critical skill: Transportation Management Specialist. He probably regretted it, but in retrospect, he was one lucky guy. The Second World War had a great impact upon all of us. Jim remembers old Mr. John Brown, white helmet and all, as our Civil defense air raid warden coming around 7630 and raising good natured hell because of Orville's leaky curtain. The confrontation could not have been too bad because the families remain close to this day.

The war was all around us. From ration cards to bond drives to war flicks to the daily drilling of the South Shore ROTC cadets we were as involved as we could be for that time. We built elaborate forts that resembled the defenses at Verdun or on the Somme in the previous war. In a way we were perhaps living out the old military dictum of the generals who were always "fighting the last war."

Military ceremonies were held with regularity on the front steps of the main entrance to South Shore High School. Honors given to those young fighting men and women from the neighborhood who were off to Africa, the Pacific or to Europe. As I remember it went on even after the war was over. It seems incredible that some of the ROTC kids we would see trying to march with some kind of regularity down Bennett, over 77th and up Constance Avenue would actually see combat. I'm sure some did. One of them was young Marv Levy, ace running back for South Shore and former head coach of the Buffalo Bills. I got a letter from him on

Bills stationary in response to my query of the memories of his days in South Shore. He gave me his dates of service in the Air Force and said that he thought I knew more about the "Old Neighborhood" than he did. I didn't of course. He was being kind. I had the advantage of the Chicago Historical Society and Phil Jordan.

EDUCATION, HIGHER EDUCATION, AND POLITICS

Education was, and still is, the key to the future generations of Shermans. "Get an education, you won't be able to do like I did!" Orv would say, like so many others in that generation. "You can take that with you wherever you go!" Another major theme for the Shermans of South Shore was politics. Family ties to politics range from the politics of Pennsylvania to the Wilson Democrats of the Dakotas and from the Martin Kennelly connection with the Allied Van Lines, to Jim's connections with Marty Russo as well as his heading up the Catholic Teachers Union and his work for the State of Illinois, Department of Corrections from 1973 to 1977.

Chicago of course is the home of the deal: "you scratch my back and I'll scratch yours." "Let's make a deal. I won't get everything I want and you won't get everything you want, but together we'll get just about everything we need." Deals were made in the growth period of South Shore from 1910 to 1940 like no other in the city, except of course that of Bridgeport, which lived on deals and politics. Our little neighborhood (not so little in actuality—more than 79,000 in the 1940 census) was known as an elite area. Not that we felt in any way superior to anyone, but we did have some interesting political connections. Old John Melaniphy became corporation counsel for the City of Chicago. The Melaniphys had a ton of kids and lived just a couple of blocks away at 77th and Ridgeland. Our classmate Elise Bundesen's father, Dr. Herman Bundesen (or as my dad always irreverently called him, Dr. "Bunionson") became head of Chicago's Public Health department. He was best known and appreciated during heat waves. He would not only issue heat alerts but would give a kind of social and medical dispensation so that men could go to work without their ties and women could dispense with their girdles. Nick Bohling was our alderman and our connection to city hall for many years and many deals. We also had Al Capone's right hand man: Murray "The Camel" Humphreys.

He lived at 7716 Bennett in a gorgeous 'Tudor-Mob' style home-fortress. In 1952 during the Republican National convention, he was visited by General Eisenhower to make a deal for support from the labor unions that Humphreys controlled. The rest, as they say, is history! When his daughter Llewella graduated from South Shore High School, the entertainment for her graduation party was flown in from Las Vegas: Old Blue Eyes himself, Frank Sinatra. How's that for clout?

The deal was that crooks didn't want to live where they "crooked." They wanted to live in a safe area like South Shore. They wanted a safe place for their families and children to grow up in. Who wouldn't?

Not that we didn't have our moments. Our classmate JoAnn Rinella's relative, Sam Rinella, was gunned down in front of his home on 78th and Chappell, just a block away from Our Lady of Peace. It was a great funeral, for those of us who got to serve as altar boys—the biggest tip we ever had!

As if all that wasn't enough, we had the distinction of being home to a number of class act newspaper men. Warren Brown from the old Chicago Herald and later the Herald American was the early dean of sportswriters when Ben Bentley was still in diapers. He was a good buddy of Father Ignatius McDermott, who remembers him fondly. Warren reputedly taught a couple of other sportswriters everything they knew: John Carmichael of the Daily News (you might recall the barber pole logo and his column "The Barber Shop"). Dave Condon of the Tribune ("In the Wake of the News") was my favorite. A good natured jolly fat guy with glasses, he lived at 78th and Bennett and was a regular paying customer on my paper route.

Except for the Guzik brothers, Paul Pierce and a few other gangsters, South Shore was a very classy place. We had it all. Location, location and more location. Near good shopping, beautiful homes, churches, schools, the lake, the IC, and the CTA (we never owned a car until 1954), prairies, theaters, and great restaurants. The Loop was less than half an hour away and there were no traffic jams then. A short hop to the north and we were in Jackson Park, the Museum of Science and Industry, and on the campus of one of the world's great universities: The University of Chicago. We even had our own South Shore Country Club, a jewel on the lake with our own golf course. We had a ballpark, Bidwell Stadium, with our own girls' professional baseball team, the Bluebirds. Who could want anything else?

WE OWNED THE WORLD

We all went on of course, in a kind of American Diaspora: Chicago Heights, Homewood, Evergreen Park, Orland Park, Crete, Park Forest, and Downers Grove. Then: Colorado, Florida, California, Wisconsin, and Michigan. It was never ever the same though. My wife says it is just our youth I am missing. That may be part of it, but we had something very special for an urban area. I have never seen its like any place or any time again to the same degree and with even similar dimensions. Take a look at Alan Ehrenhalt's wonderful book about 1957, The Lost City and you'll see what I mean.

On a Chicago Tribune bulletin board on the internet I saw a message that summed up a lot about our old neighborhood: "We owned the World" it said. I locked in on it with anticipation. It was from a Jewish couple from South Shore High School who had fallen in love, graduated, married, had children, and moved away to some faceless suburb. It wasn't arrogant at all. Wistful maybe, but it tried to express that feeling so many of us had of growing up in a place and time where we had everything we needed – a real sense of community lost.

I have come full circle in my bitterness about the loss and destruction of a beautiful neighborhood. Whites, Blacks, Catholic, Protestant or Jews, we are all just pilgrims, just traveling through. We are all just renting. What do we really own in the long run of things?

We can't live in the past. We have great things to look forward to in the future. Still, it is a good and wonderful thing to remember that even in the aftermath of the Depression, hard times and war, we could create a sense of community. No matter where we wind up on our pilgrimage we can help each other out, share our loads and look forward to a day of resurrection and reunions!

As Thomas Merton lovingly reminds us in his classic Seven Storey Mountain, "We have what we seek. We don't have to rush after it. It was there all the time, and if we give it time, it will make itself known to us."

12

RITES OF PASSAGE

"When I was a child, I spoke as a child, I understood as a child, I thought as a child; but when I became a man, I put away childish things. For now we see in a mirror, dimly, but then face to face. Now I know in part, but then I shall know just as I also am known. And now abide faith, hope, love, these three; but the greatest of these is love."

- I Corinthians Ch. 13

It seems like we have lost our appreciation of rites of passage for our young people these days. We and they are missing some kind of clear demarcation from childhood and adolescence into adulthood. Maybe it's just our hectic modern lifestyle. Perhaps it is just that our sense of community and our whole social fabric seems to be so stretched and unraveled. So many of our young people seem to be drifting without a strong sense of direction, purpose, or meaning in life.

Other religions and cultures still have a very clear line. The Hispanic "Quinceañera" is a marvelous example for their young women as are the Jewish Bar and Bat Mitzvahs. Yes, Christians have confirmation, but even that event seems to be watered down these days. A friend of mine used to say, "Our children today are suffering from the misery of unimportance." He may be on to something. How can we give our young people a sense of responsibility and belonging that we once had? We have given them material things, but all of their needs are not material.

I don't know the answer and I'm sure we cannot have all of our young people go on a vision quest. But, it seems to me there should be some kind of culminating challenge for our young ones that would help them to discover themselves, their strengths and weaknesses, and head into adulthood with a sense of meaning and purpose. Facing real challenges and overcoming them seems to be the best, indeed maybe the only, way to a successful adulthood.

A couple of years ago, my old Our Lady of Peace buddy Phil Jordan and I took a trip down south to St. Catherine's, the Dominican Mother House near Bardstown, Kentucky. While we were there, we met our old principal from our grade school in the South Shore neighborhood in Chicago. Sister DePorres, a marvelous person and administrator, was amazed and pleased to see us. We talked about some of our hair-raising adventures at Our Lady of Peace in the old days as well as some of the grand old OLP families: the Delaneys, Walls, Melaniphys, the Mahers, Figels, the Shermans and the Gerritys, among many others.

We told her about our many surreptitious trips up to the top of the great tower between the church and the school. It was hard and dangerous to a degree, particularly if one were challenged to walk around the outside top ledge about fifty feet off the ground.

Our old nun just smiled: "I knew you boys were going up there," she smiled slyly, "but I felt that boys needed a rite of passage, so I didn't have the trap doors locked, even though others felt they should be."

She was a good and wise woman and we were lucky to have had her guidance. Then I began thinking about all the other things we did that were dangerous, even foolhardy, but in the long run helped us to become men. They were, in sum, our own rites of passage. In our culture we don't have one single defining kind of celebration or ritual toward adulthood. It is a series of events, a composite of experiences leading toward becoming your own person. It is not always completed by 18 or 21, or in some cases, even later. Unfortunately, in too many cases it is never completed. It can also be lost through accidents, death or what I call "arrested maturity," or a kind of extended adolescence.

Maybe it was the war. I don't know. It seems to me now that we were given extraordinary latitude when we were young. I think that it was also related to the tenor of the times. People looked out for others, particularly children. People also held children accountable—even other people's children. For whatever reason, there was not the frequency of child abuse or the level of violence against young people that we seem to have now. There was a greater sense of community and collective responsibility.

We were really princes of the city or at least princes of the south side, or maybe in reality, just princes of South Shore, but we were able to travel, at a relatively young age, in ways that children today would never be allowed to do.

We hitched rides on about anything that moved. We would flip slow coal trains, skid behind cars in the winter, hop on delivery wagons, make homemade racing carts and soap derby cars.

It seemed to us that there was a real difference between the Irish Catholic community and the Jewish families. The Jewish kids just plain had more boundaries and supervision. By contrast, we were allowed to run a little more and take risks that the Jewish kids did not get to do.

We began hitchhiking downtown from 79th and Jeffery when we were in seventh or eighth grade. Not alone maybe, but still it was risky. I do not recall one instance of any inappropriate behavior of any adult who ever picked us up, but still.

People will say things just were not reported the way they are now. That may be true to a degree. I just think there was a different view of things and it was a simpler era. Don't forget, there was only half the population in the country compared to now. It was really a more basic, simpler kind life then.

One big thing we liked to do as early as the summer between grade school and high school was to go out to the AAA auto auction in Dyer, Indiana and drive cars back for local auto dealers. They would buy three or four of them and then needed help getting them all back. We didn't have driver's licenses, but why quibble about little things?

That was really a kind of rite of passage for us. All of a sudden we had an automobile to get back into the city. We didn't always go back the most direct route. What good would it have been to go all the way out there and not be able to swing by our favorite ice cream shop or park and pick up some of the guys (and girls, if we really got lucky)? Eventually we did get back to the dealer's lot. You could pick out the dealer. He was usually a fat, bald guy with a name like Sam or Irving or Benny and a cigar, pacing nervously in front of his car lot on South Chicago Avenue, looking at his watch and shaking his head. I think they were so glad to see us, particularly if we and the car were still in one piece, that they cooled off quickly. Typical pay was five bucks if you were lucky, nothing if you were not. However, the experience was priceless, as they say today.

Our first real date in grade school was another rite of passage for both boys and girls. I'm not talking about a group date, or a date with any parents along, but a real "just you and her and 'gulp' what do I say next?" The first part of this deal was getting up enough nerve to ask the girl out at all. Here it did help if your families lived fairly close because then you were going to be headed to or from school at times and you got to know each other a little bit along the way.

Well, I was madly in love (as much as a seventh grader can be) with a beautiful Irish colleen by the name of Kathleen Fitzgibbons. So were most of the other guys, including my classmate, Jim Sherman. But I lived closer to my dream girl, just two buildings north on Constance.

The "romantic" event was the 1950 Prep Bowl football championship of Chicago featuring our own Mount Carmel "dream team" of the Catholic League against Lane Tech, a perennial public school powerhouse whose claim to fame was to have an amusement park, old Riverview, next to its campus at Belmont and Western.

The game was being played at Soldier Field on the lake and home to all the major events of the time in Chicago. In fact, the Prep Bowl still holds the U.S. record for the most people at any sporting event of all time, including any Super Bowl. 124,000 plus filed in on an early December day in 1939 to see Leo Catholic High take on Austin.

Somehow, I got Kathleen to agree to the date and then convinced our parents as well. We took the ICRR down, which was a lot classier than the CTA, and got off at the 12th Street stop for Soldier Field. There weren't 124,000 on that day but it was still crowded. We made it down there in good time and were thrilled to see our local heroes: Tom Carey, Tim McHugh, Van Snyder , Ted Cachey, and Dan Shannon. The game started off as an even power struggle but very quickly Mount Carmel took control and the Catholic League strength began to show itself. By the time the rout was on, the weather had deteriorated and become rainy, misty and foggy. At some point, I think it happened when I went out to get some hot dogs, we got separated. I was in shock. I looked all over our area for an hour or more.

No luck! Finally, I headed for the Outer Drive and began hitchhiking home. Who pulls up but our own pastor, His Royal Highness Henry Friel, majestically sitting in the back seat of the "Monsignormobile," being driven by our school custodian, Nick Rollinger. I jumped up and down, waved my arms, yelled and screamed.

They looked at me with a look of disdain that a Rockefeller might have shown to a beggar on Fifth Avenue in New York City. The last thing I saw was the rear license plate and a cloud of exhaust.

I finally did get a ride from some rejoicing and celebrating Mount Carmel fans and got back in fairly good shape. I can't remember what happened to Kathleen after that day. I think she moved away shortly after that and I never saw her again. To this day, however, I always look at the hair-netted ladies working the food stands at Soldier Field to see if she might be there, working for old Consolidated Concessions and waiting for her long lost boyfriend.

We were lucky to have our own Lake Michigan coastline with a beautiful park and beach. Rainbow Beach. Our beach was something special. It ran from 75th Street on the north to 79th Street on the south. At the north end off 75th Street were the infamous rocks, a kind of breakwater pier of giant stone blocks extending into the lake. Sooner or later you were going to be challenged to dive, not jump, off the rocks into the uncharted dark blue waters of the lake on the north side of the rocks.

Didn't know how to swim? Too bad. "Tough titty, said the little kitty," went our little ditty. You're were gonna learn fast—or else! Many of us joined the junior lifeguards to work on our swimming skills and to learn small lifeboat handling skills. The guards had their own clubhouse, which really set us apart. The goal was to pass the qualifying swim tests to become a regular lifeguard with pay during the summer, with beautiful girls hanging all over you and admiring your great physique and tan. For most of us it was just that: a dream. Still, that first dive off the rocks was something else and another small rite of passage.

I think that sports as a whole became a kind of rite of passage for us. I always have been grateful that our folks just left us to ourselves when it came to sports and competition. There wasn't the organization that there is today. We had to put everything together ourselves. From setting up baseball diamonds, to flooding hockey rinks on the prairies, to making alley basketball courts, we did it all. As I think about it now, we learned a great deal about negotiating, diplomacy, give and take, leadership, salesmanship, organization and being able to rely on ourselves. They were great life lessons.

It was not all about play though. We were beginning to learn about work as well. Coming out of the Depression and going through World War II, money was scarce for us, and we scrambled to add a little honest cash to our pockets. We did work around our own homes and apartment buildings: washing windows, sweeping up, taking out the trash, stoking the coal furnaces. Then we began to look outside. We would help bag and carry groceries, babysit, wash cars, mow lawns, and shovel sidewalks. We would collect scrap metal for cash or for the war effort, dive for golf balls in water traps to sell at local golf courses, caddy, go caroling at Christmas time, pass out advertising flyers—in short, anything to work toward a little more independence. We didn't realize it, but we were getting ready for the next stage of life: getting a real job.

In another sense we were developing resiliency. Resiliency is that most elusive quality of being able to take the big hits in life and being able to bounce back. Not only being able to bounce back, but like a great running back, keep moving with a smile that says, "You didn't hurt me, is that all you've got?" even while hurting on the inside. There is a bit of cockiness to it, bravado or brashness to a degree, but without it you are going to have real difficulty handling the inevitable setbacks that every one of us faces in life.

The small challenges of childhood are nothing compared to the struggles and hurdles that come later: high school, college, vocational training, military service, courtship, marriage, divorce, careers, layoffs, children, deaths, disappointments and disasters. All of this comes, along with our own aging and death somewhere, somehow, sometime.

Every one of us, no matter where we are from, have to face all of this. I just give thanks that we grew up in a time and place that helped us to get through most of this and not only survive, but thrive. Now it is time, it seems to me, to pass it on in some way. Altruism. Generosity. To give to others: both the generation ahead of us and the generations to follow. We were truly and richly blessed.

"I have fought the good fight. I have completed the race. I have kept the faith."

- St. Paul in Timothy 2, 4;7

13

THE COAST OF SOUTH SHORE

"I am one of America's Great Lakes people, her fresh-water people, not an oceanic but a continental people. Whenever I swim in an ocean, I feel as though I am swimming in chicken soup."

- Kurt Vonnegut, University of Chicago

I was thinking about what the greatest single unifying element in South Shore might be as I looked back on a lifetime of connections there. It really didn't take long to discover that it was, at least for me, the coast of South Shore. It was that stretch of Lake Michigan beachfront from the old South Shore Country Club (or even a little north of that up into Jackson Park) all the way down to the overflow at 79th Street.

The steel mills were there to the south but they really were not in South Shore, although we could see them clearly from our beach, Rainbow Beach. Many people probably think it was named for the Rainbow Coalition, a south side community organization run by Jesse Jackson. Not so. It ran from 75th Street on the north to 79th Street on the south.

At the north end off 75th were the infamous rocks, a breakwater pier of giant stone blocks extending out into the lake. At some point, sooner or later, you were going to be challenged to dive, not jump, off the rocks into the uncharted dark blue waters of the lake on the north side of the rocks.

Rainbow Beach was really the centerpiece of our neighborhood. Its name reflected the pride that our fathers and grandfathers had in the U.S. Army's Rainbow Division. The Fighting 42nd of World War I fame with Douglas MacArthur was made up of troops from all over the country instead of the usual pattern of a single state or region like the 32nd (Red Arrow) Division from Wisconsin and Michigan.

As far as we were concerned, Rainbow Beach was the jewel in the crown. It was not just a beach but one of the best parks in the city. It was a four block stretch that had all we needed for recreation. There was a football field and baseball diamond at the north end of the park close to 75th Street. It was the home field of the St. Bride's grammar school team, which was one good team in its day. Tommy Harkins, Mike Savage, Porky McGrath, Ed Moriarity and Jimmy Heffernan were re-

really the class of the Catholic Youth Organization grade school league in the early fifties.

This field was also the traditional scene of the annual Turkey Bowl, played every Thanksgiving Day morning between the old guys and the young guys. This was sandlot football at its finest, with roots going directly back to the days of the flying wedge and no helmets. There were no uniforms to speak of, just hand-me-downs or leftovers stolen from various south side high schools such as Leo, Mount Carmel, South Shore, Mendel, DeLaSalle or Chicago Vocational School. As little kids we were thrilled to see our local heroes, Tom Carey, Van Snyder, Dick Prendergast, Tim McHugh, Baldy Russell, Beano McFarland and a host of others from various and sundry colleges, reform schools and semipro teams like the old Chicago Hornets.

Seems to me that the main gathering place before the game, and certainly after the game, was the Emerald Isle Tap on 75th Street just west of Exchange with

Joe the Polack, proprieter, or Joe Nietupski to you. This tavern was home to a whole host of illustrious characters and was a repository of local lore and legends.

Over by the football/baseball field was the lifeguard shack. Many us would be in the junior guards and a select few even made the regular senior guards. The junior guards was like a kind of boot camp for developing those kids who were going to be the backbone of the lifeguard program for the Chicago Park District, not only for Rainbow Beach but for quite a few of the south side beaches in the city.

About two miles out directly offshore from our beach was one of a few water department cribs. From our vantage point it looked like a replica of a Civil War ironclad, like the Monitor or the Merrimack. Only it never moved. Its main function was to draw in fresh drinking water and send it to the big water filtration plant up by Navy Pier. Crews were supplied by a "bumboat" that came out every week with food and supplies and fresh crews. It must have been a good place to work, at least in the summer, and like most city jobs, you had to know somebody to get out there. That was just the way it worked. The motto was simple: "We don't want nobody-nobody sent..." If you weren't connected to an alderman or ward committeeman, or a relative in city hall, "Forgetaboutit Pal!" "G'wan home." "Take a sneak." "Amscray!"

The area around the South Shore beaches and the park was originally developed by English and Welsh workers who were building up the area as a resort community with cottages, beach homes, and resort hotels in the 1880s to get some relief from the steamy, hot and humid Chicago summers. They were also bringing in the Illinois Central tracks off the mainline and out Exchange Avenue near the lake. Hence all the British names in the area: Chelten and Cheltenham, Windsor and Windsor Park, Bryn Mawr, and Chatham. Maybe that's why my grandfather Lewis settled into South Shore, first around 77th and Constance and later to 72nd and Clyde across from Aquinas Dominican High School for young ladies.

Rainbow Park also had tennis courts (we never used them) and four outdoor handball courts that were in use from early morning until dark seven days a week, at least in the summer. They were three-wall wooden rectangles on a concrete slab with the back open and a chicken wire ceiling. I've played in other cities over time, but I have never seen their like again.

The basic rule was that as long as you won, you held the court. Good players could hold the court for hours, and on a hot day you could drop 5-8 pounds easily. Handball was in our blood for some reason, somehow particularly with the Irish. Every firehouse in the neighborhood had an indoor court that was open to the public as long as the firemen were not playing. We had year-round free facilities and there was nothing better than a good game of handball doubles followed by a cool swim in Lake Michigan before drying off on the 75th Street rocks and working on your tan!

We thought we owned the world. It just didn't get any better than that.

The lake and Rainbow Beach became the center of our universe, at least for three seasons: baseball, football, and basketball. We practically grew up at the park and the beach. Early on my family lived at 78th and Coles. Coles was as far east as you could go in Chicago, at that point anyway. I have tons of old black and white Kodak Brownie snapshots of us at the park, the beach, and the lake—right out our back door into the park and beach.

Even when we moved further west, we were always drawn as though by a magnet to our own gold coast: to Rainbow Beach and Lake Michigan. This love affair has lasted a lifetime. Even when we moved up to Wisconsin in 1975, where did we go but to Sheboygan and into an old white house almost within sight of the big lake. We lived there almost 30 years.

Likewise, my wife, Peggy's family moved to Michigan after the war and up to the Sleeping Bear Sand Dunes area near Traverse City. Guess where? Her aunt and uncle right on Lake Michigan itself, and her grandparents within sight of the lake in Glen Haven. We have taken the Badger Auto Ferry over to Michigan and back to Wisconsin more times than we care to count, including our honeymoon in August of 1966. Now that is a cheap date, albeit a memorable time!

My brother John, my nephew Dominick, and the indomitable "Captain" Ernie Collins, and I were in the Chicago to Mackinac sailboat race one summer. At least we were until we became becalmed in Pentwater, Michigan. It was still a great experience while it lasted and I will never forget taking the helm at two in the morning, looking out and seeing the great racing boats all around all around us heading north-northeast under a fast wind, a near full moon and a cool starry sky.

My other experience with Lake Michigan involved shipping out of South Chicago as a young man on one of the big Great Lakes ore carriers.

I was never a coal miner, but I have sure had some experience with coal. When I was young and a bit adventurous, I signed on the Great Lakes Ore Carriers. I soon found out why I got on so easily. The only job open was the worst one, a coal passer. The picture above is one of the boats I was on, the Frank R. Denton.

The ore boats are big, some 300-400 feet long. They ran back and forth from Lake Superior down to the steel mills on the other Great Lakes. On the old boats, the engines ran on coal, not diesel like they do now, so most of the time we had to keep the coal hoppers filled, which wasn't too bad because they had automatic stokers. Eventually, though, the coal bunkers started to get empty. Then the fun began. The coal would get stuck high up against the corners of the bunker, and the bunkers themselves were quite high. We were working more than three stories down below the waterline. The word was that if the ship ever rolled over in a storm, we would never be able to get out like the deck hands way above us. Cheerful thought!

Anyhow, when the iron stoker could not bring in any coal, somebody, usually the newest guy, had to climb into the bunkers and pull the coal down with a long-handled steel rake from the corners to where it could be picked up by the stoker screws in the bottom of the coal bunker. Fun job! It was especially fun when the ship was rolling in bad weather, and you were seasick on top of everything else.

That was bad enough, but it was really something when the old mechanical stokers broke down, which was often. Then the work really started. Those shifts changed to two hours on and four off. The heat was terrific: 100 degrees minimum and sometimes 120 degrees or hotter. All the coal had to be shoveled in by hand then, and the clinkers had to be taken out manually with long steel tongs. Nobody had their shirts on, and you would be completely soaking wet in about ten minutes. We wore bandannas on our foreheads to keep the sweat out of our eyes. They had salt tablets for us and some hoses with fresh water to spray ourselves off with from time to time when we got too hot. The old timers said you could lose ten pounds in a shift, and I believed them.

We would work two hours and then have four hours to get something to eat and catch a bit of sleep in our bunk. One good thing was that the food on those ore boats was really good and there was plenty of it because we were never long out of port. You got your ten pounds back in a hurry!

The thing that I cannot get away from now is a sense of linkage from both a historical and a geographical perspective. Lake Michigan and Rainbow Beach were linked to all the other Great Lakes and the Illinois River down the Mississippi to the Gulf of Mexico.

That is quite a bit of land and water to be connected to, as well as much of the history of this country. Likewise, we are all somehow connected to each other, but we miss those connections all the time unless we make the effort to look deeper and ask the right questions. We just have to do it before it's too late and all the memories disappear, forever.

14

PLANES, TRAINS, AND AUTOMOBILES: THE MUSEUM

There was only one museum for us in South Shore: The Museum of Science and Industry. It was virtually in our South Shore neighborhood, located at the north end of Jackson Park on the lake. Of all the museums in Chicago, this was number one for us. It was where our grandparents and parents would take us when we were young. It was where we would play hooky on rainy days. It was our refuge from boredom in the dog days of August and in the frigid winter days with the relentless winds howling the "below zeros" off the lake and up our wazoos.

It was a real jewel, and I won't bore you with the details of the place. You'll just have to go there yourself. Don't forget to notice the Greek ladies holding the roof up with their heads. They've never moved since I was a spring chicken.

The other museums were snootier, some even prettier, but actually more boring. This museum was a real hands-on deal where you could explore, hustle, play, think, and get involved with as much as you wanted.

It was originally the palace of something or other during the Columbian Exposition of 1893. When the other temporary exhibits were torn down or fell down over time, the building was redone into the structure it is today. My history and relationship with that building goes back to my own beginning. I was born across the street at the old Illinois Central Hospital on Stony Island Avenue and have stayed connected with the museum over the years.

I have no idea when I made my first visit, but I do remember being there with my Hannan grandparents around four or so. They laughed for years at the memory of me standing in the cab exhibit of a steam locomotive that was disconnected from the boiler and connected to the wall. I reportedly looked up at it wide-eyed and said, "I wish I had my "wittle" toolbox." Looking at all the nuts and bolts in that cab made me want to take it apart. It was definitely a hands-on place, unlike the other museums where you were constantly told "stay off this or that," or "don't touch," or "get down!" At our museum we were constantly encouraged not only to look but to touch, turn, crank, spin, dial, whisper, laugh, hold, and move; in short, we were told to explore. In fact, it really should have been called an "exploratory" because that was what it was. And explore we did, probably including some areas that were not really designed to be explored either.

As you walked in the imposing art deco entrance on the north side off 57th Street, you were immediately awed, at least I was, by the British Supermarine Spitfire hanging overhead in a frozen dogfight with a German Stuka dive bomber. We kids would get cricks in our necks as we stood there for what seemed like hours watching the imaginary air battle. Eventually, we would get shuffled off by the incoming crowds to a stairway where we would head upstairs so we could look down on the model railway train and get our necks unkinked. We were transfixed, or maybe "trainsfixed."

The 9500 square foot model train set was certainly one of the largest sets in the world and led to my request for my own set, which my grandfather Hannan promptly went home to his Wizards workshop and duplicated a smaller version. It was mounted on two 4x8 reinforced sheets of plywood that were buckled together so it could be easily stored no matter how small the apartment was that we were in. I remember that it was an American Flyer set, and Papa, who was quite an artist as well as an electrical genius, hand painted the entire set and made all of the houses, towns, bridges, electric gates, farms and stores with interior lights, bells and whistles. I was the hit of the neighborhood, a junior Casey Jones!

We never had a definite pattern for going through the museum. We went whichever way our minds and feet wandered and where the crowds were thinnest. Like a magnet, at some point we always headed for the coal mine, which was a favorite with all the kids and a few grownups too. When you went down the shaft, it felt like you were going a mile down. The thing was you always forgot that you had just climbed up two stories just to get down the elevated shaft. It clanged and banged all the way into the basement someplace, shaking and rattling all the way. It was always worth the wait, and there always was a wait. The tunnel ride that you switched to after you got to the bottom was exciting. Pitch black and bumpy, you were jerked and twisted back and forth. It was a great place to take a date later on or even if you were lucky enough to pick up some girls, this was the place to sneak a quick squeeze, or at least 'test the waters'.

I can't remember where the tracks went, probably in a figure eight, until you wound up in the mine itself where you got to see the drilling equipment in operation and see a Davy lamp exhibition as well as get a lecture about modern coal mining. Most of us were just glad that we were never going to have to work in the mines, particularly those of us with English or Welsh backgrounds, where we had heard about the mines from our parents and grandparents.

PLANES, TRAINS, AND AUTOMOBILES: THE MUSEUM

Time to move along. Let's go see the farm. Plastic cows and styrofoam pigs were watched by fake horses and improbable stuffed chickens, but it didn't bother us any. We had never seen a better farm and probably wouldn't for many years if ever.

We headed down and out to see the old U-505 submarine. I had seen it come across Lake Shore Drive by Jackson Park Beach when they brought it to the museum. That was an exciting day and all night operation. Our favorite submarine movie of all time was Das Boot, which we saw in German at (appropriately) the Downer theater in Milwaukee. The German studio that was doing the film had come over to Chicago to get the dimensions and details for the movie U-Boat because it was, and still is, the only boat still in usable condition. I remember the blue and white checkered sheets on the bunks of the crew members, and those were duplicated precisely in the movie.

I remember when I was a kid, everything was connected to WWII and the museum had tons of wartime stuff, including films of all the Marine amphibious operations in the Pacific. We kids would watch those for what seemed to be hours on end in the museum basement.

The exhibits are not all remembered for being spectacular. Some were downright spooky. One that got me was the iron lung. Polio was a real scourge in those days, but it's almost unheard of now. Back then it was a very real deal. Even President Roosevelt was crippled from it. My younger brother Donnie contracted it very early on and was crippled from it, as well as having Muscular Dystrophy. Talk about a double whammy! For some reason, I always remembered that iron lung exhibit with a mixture of fear and horror. The idea of spending the rest of my life in that contraption was just too much for me. I would always avoid that exhibit like the plague.

The other exhibit that was just plain gruesome to me but did have a certain amount of macabre fascination and dark humor was Granny, the Delicatessen Lady. She had been a real person somewhere and must have been related to a real family. Somehow her body wound up in a medical research facility and was preserved. That was bad enough, but then they sliced her longways into thin, perfectly even slices. Actually, I think that she was black, not that it made any difference or even that you could really tell from the inside. Maybe that was the lesson.

Al's Beef could not have done a better job of slicing. They took each slice and laminated it between hard plastic sheets. The sheets were then mounted to a hinged display rack that could be opened like the pages of a book. Some book! Not exactly bedtime reading.

The only good thing was, it was a great place to take those girls you were trying to pick up. The deal was to gross them out with Granny and then take them to the Colleen Moore dollhouse, which was cool, dark and beautiful. Then you could get things back together again and maybe sneak a kiss or two in the process.

The best time of the year was Christmas time. The museum was always nice and warm. We loved the display in the lobby of the Christmas trees from around the world. No one had ever seen so many beautifully decorated trees, each one lavished with the best ornaments from that particular country: Poland, England, Lithuania, Scandinavia, Germany, France and Italy. I don't know if they still do this now. It's probably too politically incorrect or something.

PLANES, TRAINS, AND AUTOMOBILES: THE MUSEUM

I think that even the Jewish families and children enjoyed the stunning display. I believe that many of the Jews, at least in South Shore and Hyde Park, observed the holidays as a secular time of giving. When you think about it, it is a universal need for all of us, regardless of religion, creed or what have you.

One of my favorite places of all in the museum, particularly during the holiday season, was the Street of Yesteryear. It was a real blast from the past for us kids and gave us an idea of our grandparents' younger days. I wonder if someday they will have an updated version that would be set in the fifties.

In any event, we loved the old time movie house, which even had an old lady playing an old piano along with the old silent movies. Later on it was just a recording but we liked to hear the real thing. There were horseless carriages parked in front of the old stores and Christmas decorations galore.

I remember when I was teaching special education kids at Bloom High School in the mid-60s. EMH was what the students were called then: Educable Mentally Handicapped. We keep changing what we call them so I don't know what it is any more. Somehow I got permission to take my class of 12 kids to the museum for a field trip. Actually, they did not seem to mind my kids being out of the building. That was exactly what I had in mind anyway because I always felt that kids with this kind of disability should be out in the community as much as possible. "Learning by the soles of their shoes," my old supervisor at Illinois State, Dr. Bill Zbinden, used to say.

I prepped them as much as I could and we reviewed safety rules and the need to stay together and so on. We did have one guy that really worried me. Bobby was the nicest kid you would ever hope to meet. Unfortunately, he was totally discombobulated. Besides the basic level of retardation, he had a host of other difficulties such as vision problems, hearing difficulties, speech problems and severe epilepsy. When problems were handed out, let's just say that Bobby got more than his fair share. The one that worried me the most was the problem with seizures. We had the school nurse come in and review all the procedures we should be aware of if Bobby had a seizure. We went over many other first aid situations as well.

We got to the museum on a beautiful late spring day. I was tempted to take them all out through Jackson Park but then thought better of it. I had some student helpers along and two parents as well. We were going all over the building when Bobby got out of my group and went off with the other group. I didn't worry too much at first but thought I'd better try to find out where they were, just in case.

All of a sudden one of the kids from the other group came running up for me. "Mr. Lewis, Mr. Lewis! Bobby's had a seizure, but don't worry we're taking care of it and everything's OK." OK, I thought, how could it all be OK? I took off like a shot and followed the kid through what seemed like miles of exhibits, hallways and staircases. I came around a corner by the Foucault pendulum and there were all the kids from the second group sitting on a bench their backs against the marble wall.

"Where's Bobby?" I croaked. "Don't worry, Mr. Lewis, he's not shaking anymore." All of a sudden I wasn't worried about the shaking, I was worried about his breathing. They had rolled him against the wall and were nonchalantly sitting on him, coolly looking around in all directions, people and kids walking every which way and no one with even the slightest idea that this poor kid was squashed under half of his classmates. The kids were right. He wasn't shaking. He wasn't breathing any too good either. I did some CPR and he began to show some color and eventually came out of it OK. Then I needed some CPR.

Peggy and I were married near the museum at the Unitarian Church on 57th and Woodlawn in August 1966 at the beginning of the real cranking-up of President Johnson's War in Vietnam. The night before the wedding I received an apologetic phone call from the assistant minister, Rev. Paul Hanchett. After much hemming and hawing, I finally got the information that our regular minister would not be able to officiate at the ceremony because he had been arrested at the Museum of Science and Industry for chaining himself to the front doors in protest of an army exhibit that was due to open that weekend.

In retrospect, I give him a lot of credit. I wish that I had been more active against the war that cost us 58,000 deaths and who knows how many more casualties, many still going on now and will be for a long time to come. But that was then and this is now. As Kurt Vonnegut, a local in the neighborhood, would say, "So it goes."

I go back to the museum now, not as often as I would like, but from time to time to take my grandchildren and thus add another generation to the club. Somehow, it's just not the same. I guess that is an obvious statement when you think about it. The exhibits are all updated, as they should be. It would be awful if after 70 years nothing had changed. The other thing is that I have changed. I think that's the real difference. The great thing is that the museum itself is still there. It changes to meet the times, of course, and that is as it should be but it feels good to know that in our throw-away society, there is one constant. Good to know that the Foucault pendulum is still keeping time. Good to know the museum is still there too.

PS: If you have not read David Mamet's classic: "The Museum of Science and Industry Story" in 'Chicago Stories', see if you can find it. It is both a wacky and wonderful visit to a real Chicago landmark.

15

LET'S GO TO THE MOVIES

Every small town in America had to have its picture show. South Shore was no exception. More than a small town now, South Shore had grown to almost 80,000 people by 1940. We had a variety of theaters to choose from, all within walking distance if we wanted, or just taken the old "Red Rockets," a great name for the classic red trolley car with changeover wicker seats, a "cow catcher" wood bumper, a motorman, and a conductor.

There was the Chelten Theater at 79th and Exchange. The Chelten was the original low budget show. Nondescript in its decor, it was pure function: movie screen and seats, none too comfortable. It was a great place for Saturday morning entertainment. For 25 cents you had a world of excitement on a Saturday morning with a decidedly Polish flavor and aroma. You didn't need Roger Ebert to tell you what to see either. You knew because you read the Legion of Decency in the Chicago Diocese's "The New World".

You also knew because they told you last Saturday. The cliffhanger of the week always followed the same line: good guy, Tom Mix or Johnny Weissmuller, doing battle against the forces of evil. He was always in a jam, particularly at the end of the reel, with Indians or cannibals in the deepest Congo. A beautiful girl somehow was seriously in deep doo-doo and was always rescued at the last minute. I think we booed at this, so you can tell what stage of preadolescent development we were in at the time.

I remember seeing Lon Cheney Jr. in the Mummy series at the Chelten, and also a lot of the Abbot and Costello films. The Chelten was definitely low-budget and second run. Didn't bother us any—we were kind of low budget and second-run kids. The Chelten had one drawing card over all the rest: the snooty Southtown, the royal Avalon, the understated Hamilton, the pretentious Capitol, and the "wannabe" Jeffery.

Across the street, on the west side of Exchange Ave., was a genuine Chicago-style prairie. Only this prairie was special indeed. Somebody had bought, or stolen, or maybe the military had just stored, a number of amphibious vehicles. In any event, olive and pea green amphibious tracks or ducks, Jeeps, landing barges, and half-track vehicles were all parked with more or less military precision in the vacant lot across from the Chelten theater.

Who needed fantasy on the screen when we had reality across the street? I suspect that some of those ducks were headed for amphibious operations in the Wisconsin Dells, carrying out assaults with Chicago tourists against what was left of the Menominees. We had a great time playing on that equipment! Who needed a playground or John Wayne when we had the real stuff that had been to the Pacific and back?

The Ray Theater near 75th and Exchange was also a kind of low-rent theater. It was very similar in layout to its cousin, the Chelten. We didn't go there often because it just wasn't in our "sphere of operations" at the time, although I got there more often when I began hanging around East 75th Street in high school. Ditto to the Shore Theater at 75th and Kingston. Nice, but both were definitely more Kosher than not.

The Hamilton was a step up. Located at 71st and Paxton, it related to the St. Phillip Neri crowd—folks you might caddy for at the South Shore Country Club. We saw the original Diabolique there. That kept us awake for a few nights after. This was later because it came out when we were in high school, around 1955. The Hamilton was in an understated, elegant class of its own, a lot like the country club, which gave a lot of its character to our area. We, of course, were not of that world except as caddies, busboys, lifeguards and groundskeepers.

The Jeffery was special in its own way. Much smaller than the Avalon, it certainly tried to give the grande dame Avalon a run for her money. Nicely located at 71st and Jeffery, it was in the center of the best commercial area we had. 79th was more our terrritory, but 71st Street was something special. It was a real step up, you might say.

When you went to these theaters you knew you were in a different world. You usually dressed up to at least school day standards, even Sunday duds if you had a date with, gulp, a girl. I remember hanging around Moline's one Saturday morning and overhearing one of the big guys stating kind of casually that a girl had gotten "felt up" the night before in the balcony at the Avalon. I was outwardly kind of cool and calm. Inwardly I was in a perplexed state of panic. Was she alright? Could this happen to me? What were her parents going to do about it? Who felt her up, and how,where, why, and when? Would it be in the papers? Would somebody we knew be arrested? Most importantly: WHO WAS SHE!

They all talked the same way when we were around (or maybe even when we weren't around). The sentences were composed of words that ran together. "D'nworrybouitkid" somebody said out the side of his mouth, "Y'rtooyungfordis." Then off they went to a ball game in somebody's jalopy somewhere, leaving us to figure out the mystery.

The most exciting thing about the Avalon was the planning and execution of sneaking in. Nothing, not a ball game, a dance, a streetcar, or a party, was worth it unless you could get in for free. This challenge took a ton of cunning, daring, nerve and luck. In the case of the Avalon, one preferred mode was the "Trojan Horse in Reverse." We would all chip in the cost of one ticket,

25 cents, and then send in one guy to wait for the opportune moment. He would open one of the pre-selected exit doors in the back alley. We would come piling in of course, split up immediately, and head for various seats all over the show. The ushers would come looking for us but we could throw them off if they confronted us because we usually found old ticket stubs that were hard to read in the dark, even in the glow of their flashlights.

That method was the most direct and really the most fun. Nevertheless, the other one had its moments as well. This was right up there with the Academy Awards. We would wait until the first show would be getting out, then casually walk in backwards through the crowd. You took a bit of bumping and jostling, but it was highly effective. Soon as you reached the lobby you could turn around and as nonchalantly as possible, amble on into the show of shows: the Arabian mosque of the South Side!

This whole piece reminds me of Cinema Paradiso, my all-time favorite foreign movie. It won the Academy Award for best foreign flick of 1990, so it still is not all that old. Subtitled, of course, it follows the fortunes of a small town and its theater in southern Italy through the films shown there over the years. We could have followed the fortunes of South Shore in much the same way through the local movie houses and the films they were showing at the time.

I went by the Avalon years ago. Probably the last time I ever went back to the old neighborhood. At that time it was an Evangelical black church and they were advertising a flea market fund raiser on the shattered marquee. I thought they should have blown it up like they did in Cinema Paradiso. Considering the architecture, you'd think the Black Muslims would have bought it. They must've gotten a better deal on the old Greek Orthodox church on Stony Island, I guess.

Well, surprise surprise,they did me one better. They've completely restored the place back to its "glory days" grandeur. Now it's the New Regal Theater, named after the old Regal on 47th Street that was built in the same year as the Avalon: 1927. The old Regal was no slouch either. Built to resemble a Louis XIV palace, the talent there was spectacular. Duke Ellington, Cab Calloway, Satchmo and the Mills brothers all performed there, or so I've been told.

One thing though, I bet they didn't put the swans back in the fountain at the Avalon. A sure swan song for swan soup if they did! So while you can't exactly go back again, I've talked to liberal white folks who tell me that you can safely go to events at the Avalon. Keep an eye out for something playing there that you'd like to see and I'll meet you there! On second thought, you go ahead and let me know how it went!

16

COMING TO THE PROMISED LAND

South Shore and Our Lady of Peace parish have been in our history for a long time. Our parents, aunts and uncles, and grandparents had roots there, and some of our families had been in the area since the turn of the century. We graduated from OLP in 1952 and most of us had gone on to high school, the service, college, work, marriage and families of our own without any reason to return except for nostalgia. The bittersweet memories persisted along with a feeling of discontent because the entire culture of the old neighborhood had changed, and we really could not 'go home again'. Childhood romances, schoolyard battles, "Slaughteration," ledge ball, line ball, 16 inch softball, baseball, and Catholic Youth Organization football, altar boys, The New World Catholic newspaper, low masses, high masses and novenas, climbing the tower—all were gone now except for the memories.

The neighborhood really changed in the 1960s. Black people we never dreamed of were moving up on the Illinois Central line and in old jalopies in droves. The exodus to Chicago, to "the promised land" was hitting proportions of up to a thousand people a day.

Packed into tenements in old Bronzeville around 31st and Cottage Grove, and sleeping six, seven or more to a room, something had to give. It did. The white-black boundaries inexorably changed: 35th Street, Pershing Road, 47th Street, 55th, 63rd, 71st, and finally 79th Street and beyond. It sounded like a train schedule for the IC itself and we were at the end of the line. It became a continuing flood of black humanity pushing out to the south and the west of the central city.

"I was in the Navy going to school in Memphis in 1954. No wonder the black folks wanted out of there. I also worked for the Illinois Central Rail Road at 12th Street in Chicago in 1953. We used to call the train that came in from New Orleans, "The African Queen." It would arrive late at night and 98% of the passengers were black.

In recent years I have thought of those poor folks who were mostly rural people from a warmer climate arriving late at night in the cold big city of Chicago. How confused and frightened they must have been. I do not make excuses for their behavior, but I think I understand where their hate of the white people comes from. At that time, I was told the southern states did not have unemployment or welfare funds. They would buy the folks tickets and send them north. That is what wrecked South Shore."

- Jim McGreal, OLP '51:

Hyde Park with its solid anchor of the University of Chicago became, and still is, a kind of integrated island in the stream. Then the other local neighborhoods and their parishes changed one after the other: Kenwood, Washington Park, Lawndale, Austin, Woodlawn, Grand Crossing, Englewood, and finally South Shore.

After some initial resistance, panic set in. The price of homes sold by whites dropped and the corresponding sale to a black family would be made many times at outrageously high and unfair levels. Crooked and unethical realtors made small fortunes using people against each other and playing upon everyone's fears, both white and black.

No question about it. We should have stayed and given true integration a chance. However, it turned out to be just as the old maverick Saul Alinsky defined it once. "Integration in Chicago," he observed, "is the period between the time the first black moves in and the last white moves out!" It was neither a slow nor a natural process. It was more like a tsunami, with waves of massed immigrants from the south coming on like lemmings, swamping everything in sight.

Ironic. The first black families in our neighborhood, aided by the Urban League, the NAACP and the Daily Defender were the cream of the crop: doctors, lawyers, professionals of all kinds. They were teachers, ministers, small business folks, social workers, cops and city workers just like we were or wanted to be. Unfortunately, the dregs were not far behind: the gang bangers, drug dealers, minor hoodlums and pimps along with the assorted trash and never-do- wells. We just weren't smart enough to know the difference: we thought if they looked the same, they were the same.

My eyes were opened the night we went over to move Murph out of Timmy McNamara's old house at 7710 S. Paxton. (Our first business: Pacific Movers: "For a peaceful move call Pacific!") We sat on the front porch planning our strategy for the next day's move to Downers Grove. Murph's neighbor from across the street came over. He was a physician at South Shore hospital. The first person of color on that block was coming over to bid Murph farewell.

"Murph," he said slowly and sadly, "I'm sorry to see you go! You've been a real good neighbor." He kind of paused, then stunned me with his next rueful comment: "You know, we're going to have to be moving soon too because of all these damn niggers moving in here."

It shocked me at first to hear a colored person, especially an obviously well educated and respected one, use the "N" word. Then suddenly I understood what he meant. In an odd way he was a kind of prophet to Martin Luther King. He was talking in a very pithy and practical way of judging folks not by the color of their skin but by their content, character and their actions.

It dawned on me at this point that this was not a black versus white issue but rather a class issue. I became painfully aware that it was more about moral content as opposed to pigmentation. It was about common virtues and common values as opposed to dress, looks and physical appearances.

As the struggle went on, it began to dawn on us that the majority of blacks did not want integration. That was not the real issue. The real issue was that they wanted it all, simple as that. In all fairness, however, many whites were not looking at integration either.

Over time I did begin to realize that I had a lot more in common with a middle class black educator than I did with a white redneck from Appalachia or over around the 'Bush area near Bessemer Park and the steel mills in South Chicago. These realities were a long way away when we were renting moving trucks and fighting the gangs backward block by block.

So, the "old dump" is really closed. OLP. Our old school. Hard to believe. Somehow it's easier to accept in many ways now. We and the blacks in South Shore probably are more alike than different if we pay attention to the character rather than to the characters. At least the church will go on with some good people and as long as it is there, we will still be connected to the old neighborhood!

17

OLD RIVERVIEW PARK, THE DUNKERS, AND THE TUNNEL OF LOVE

"There used to be a thing called "The African Dip." You threw balls and if you hit the target a Negro fell from his perch into the water. They got rid of the thing when Negroes learned how to throw things back. But to delay the Parachute confrontation, I once knocked the same guy into the water 23 times. The effect of that on my youthful conscience contributed to my liberal tendencies, I'm sure."

- Mike Royko

You would have thought he was an elderly black man by his shuffling walk, his stooped shoulders, his nondescript thrift shop clothing. He was a black man but he wasn't that old. He walked past a group of young, skinny black girls jumping rope on a piece of sidewalk that wasn't broken. They were screaming with laughter and high spirited good humor. He watched and listened to them for a bit as they moved like black lightning: "Cadillac, Cadillac, Cadillac car...We is smarter than you think we ....is!" They screamed and George laughed. Reminded him of his girls when they were little a long time ago down in Mississippi. He let himself into his small, bare, walkup apartment over West Side Liquors in Chicago near Western and Harrison.

The light was none too good, but he fumbled around until he found the light switch and dissipated the gloom. Eventually he lit a candle. He enjoyed the flickering light and had a candle at almost every supper meal whether he was alone or with company. It was Monday now, Monday night, and his woman-friend Rosa usually came over on Mondays because Riverview was closed that day.

When things had been good and everything was humming they were open all week. The times were changing now and little things were being cut back. No more bonuses, tips were drying up, and gangs were running in the park, particularly at night. More troubles, more police, more problems. There were fewer and fewer white people coming at night, and not that many during the day for that matter. He wondered why things just couldn't stay the same. All things changed, he knew that, but why couldn't things just stay good a little while longer? At least long enough to see his dream come true.

He lit the candle stub that was left from last night. The flare caught him a little by surprise but as it lit up the little efficiency apartment he could see his books. He didn't have many books but he did have what he considered a collection. He had a Bible, of course and he had some of Mr. Faulkner's books, some bound too, not all paperbacks. Had a copy of Tobacco Road and one big book he was very proud of: Look Homeward, Angel by Mr. Thomas Wolfe. That author wasn't from Mississippi, but he was from the south, and the writing made him feel back at home, with familiar rhythms, echoes, smells, history, family. It kept him from getting too homesick and yet made him ache for home, particularly now, in the springtime. When the park was just cranking up and the kids were not out of school yet but the days were getting longer and the rides were being tested daily with sandbags. Sandbags instead of people.

He liked Richard Wright's books and had some Walt Whitman too, Carl Sandburg, an old copy of Moby Dick that he had found on the IC train coming up that someone had left in a hurry, he guessed. He'd been afraid the porter was going to say something about it or even make him turn it in, in case there was a claim later, but the brother let it go and George began reading it that evening on the train. "Call me Ishmael," it began. He liked that. Poetic, he thought. Poetic justice. Just like his trip to Chicago during the war. One real favorite was Walden Pond by Thoreau. He only read a little bit of that at a time because it was so rich. Like the sugar molasses cookies that his grandmother used to make for him back in Mississippi. He made those last as long as he could by just taking a small bite at a time and then putting the rest away for later in the day.

George, at heart, was a deeply spiritual man. He studied the Bible regularly and talked about it to everyone he met. He had told Rosa, but not too many other folks, that his real ambition in life was to be a minister. He enjoyed working with and helping people. He did not need much money himself as his wants and needs were always somehow in balance. George was a good talker, but even more important, he was a good listener. He had a feel for people and loved them all, saints and sinners. When it came right down to it he was more interested in working with the sinners. There were more of them and they were generally more fun to be around. More real for sure.

He had left the old homestead, just a sharecropping place really, because he had heard that there was money, real money, to be made in Chicago because of the war. Later on they would be sending people up there because they had gotten into trouble or ran out of money, whatever. They just bought them a one-way ticket to the big city and dumped them in the middle of the night off the Illinois Central railroad at the 12th Street station in that cold dark city. The city was cold even in the summer, with winds blowing off the cold lake.

George knew that all warmth does not come from outer sources but the best comes from inner human goodness and kindness and a little looking after each other. That was later. Right now he was going to enjoy his night off. Right now he was going to do some reading. Rosa would be here soon. She always brought cooked barbeque ribs with all the fixin's. Wouldn't be too long now. He was looking forward to it.

It seemed a lifetime since he had left Prismatic. Little Prismatic, Mississippi, just north of Meridian. His friend had come up from Meridian and given him a lift to the IC station in Jackson. All he had, including his book collection, was packed in three boxes. Old clothesline was wrapped around each box, providing security as well as an all-purpose handle, easy to lift and sling around when you needed to do so. There were little groups of colored folks on the platform at Jackson waiting for the northbound "City of New Orleans" headed to Chicago, saying their goodbyes like other emigrants all through history.

Odd thing, he thought, during the Civil War a host of Confederate prisoners had gone to Chicago this way. Same tracks maybe. They were shipped up to Chicago to old Camp Douglas right at 35th Street and the lake. Lake Michigan. Winter and summer. Better to come up during the summer. Greater chance of surviving that way. A whole lot of the men didn't make it. They died by the hundreds and were transported to Oakwood Cemetery about 30 blocks south. Some 4000 young boys and men are buried there today in one big mound. Not many people go there any more. Things change.

George Washington (for Washington Carver) Duncan headed north. He had friends who were already working on the Northwest side of Chicago and he got a job in a plant making all kinds of armament for the war. He did well for himself. There was plenty of overtime pay and not too much time to spend it if a man was careful. The war years went well but then it was over and not too long after the VE day and then the VJ day celebrations, things began to slow down. Then, by 1950 they almost stopped altogether. Layoffs and callbacks for a time, then layoffs and no callbacks.

It was odd job time. A man took anything he could get: cleaning windows, loading freight, cooking, dishwashing, setting pins, whatever. That was when George heard about Riverview Park.

Riverview was the biggest and the best of all the amusement parks around. It was our first Magic Kingdom, so to speak, and we got there any way we could and any time we could. Somehow, George heard that Riverview was hiring and he headed out there for an application and interview. Even from a distance on the Western Avenue trolley, he could see the tops of the Pair-O-Chutes parachute tower, then the water slides, then the BOBS! BOBS was the most famous roller coaster in the Middle West. He was getting excited about his prospects as he always had been interested in railroads, machinery and in running mechanical things.

He found the office and picked up an application from a clerk who was almost asleep after lunch on a warm, drowsy spring day. He went over to the picnic grounds to fill it all out and when he brought it back to the office, the clerk was a lot more awake and even interested. "Please wait here" she asked, and went to get the foreman. Soon a big burly guy showed up. He seemed to talk mostly by growling and grunting. He also mumbled a lot and George was having difficulty understanding him. He did start to get the idea. The Polish foreman wasn't asking him about running rides. He was asking him to be part of a carnival show called the African Dip down on the Bowery near the Flying

Saucer. All George had to do was show up on time and get into a huge water tank. He would sit on a collapsible wooden seat and then tease the sailors and young guys into buying and throwing more baseballs at a bright colored metal paddle attached to the outside of the tank. When you hit the paddle, the seat collapsed and George would drop down about three feet into the water to the delight of the raucous crowd.

George was stunned. This looked embarrassing. Foolish. He started to leave and put his head down as he looked for the exit where he had come in. He heard a voice behind him. It was the little clerk from the office. "Mr. Duncan, Mr. Duncan, please stop a minute." She seemed a little embarrassed. "Mr. Duncan, I want to apologize to you!" George stopped. Never before in his life, at least not in Mississippi, had a woman, especially a white woman, apologized for anything, and from George's point of view there had been a whole lot of things to be sorry for.

"I know what you're thinking, and I agree with you that it's shameful and degrading even, but if you take this job, I will do all I can do to get you an operator's job when one comes open. Another thing, this job may not look like very much but you can make over two hundred dollars a week."

George thought for a second or two. "Two hundred dollars a week?" He couldn't believe it. Back home in old Prismatic, Mississippi it would be hard to make two hundred dollars a month chopping cotton or doing odd jobs. Maybe this was a sign. Maybe this was the Promised Land after all. Maybe he just had to get his priorities straight. He was thinking.

"What exactly to I have to do," he asked quietly. "Well, Mr. Duncan, all you have to do is something that might be hard to do at first and that is to aggravate the young white men who come out to spend a few bucks and impress their girlfriends. You get to call them names and joke around with them. The more you can rile them up, the worse their aim becomes and the more balls they'll buy to make sure they really dunk you!"

"So, in effect," she added, "you'll be an actor. You are playing a role and getting them to keep pumping more money into the game. Do you think you can do that? Will you give it a try?"

George nodded his head with a small smile. "I've been actin' all my life," he said quietly. "Down south. Actin' happy when I was cryin' inside, actin' like a servant when I was shamed, actin' cheerful when I was insulted an' abused. So, I guess I can just keep on actin' all over again."

So that was how George got to be a "dunker" in the African Dip show. He got darn good at it too. Dressed in his gray/blue pinstripe coveralls, he would really act insulting. If the guy was thin, he'd call him a toothpick. If he was heavy, he became a meatball.

He'd yell out to the guy, "Hey sucker, that ain't the gal you was wit' yesterday! What you do wit' her, man? She throw you over or sumpin'?" He would laugh his rich baritone laugh. "Hee, hee hee. Haw, Haw. You can't hit sheehit no how!"

"You ain't nuthin' but a jellyroll man, nuthin' but a real jellyroll. Hee hee. Haw haw, haw..." The sailors and the young punks would start to lose their tempers and cuss George out but good. They would call him every name in the book, most of them unprintable. The good thing was they kept on buying balls. George just kept on with the cheerful insults: "Oh man, you ain' nuthin' but a lowdown mammy lover! A real sissy one, it looks to me. Come on, mammywhammer, come on, you can't touch me!"

George's good natured patter seemed to amuse most customers. But some of the rougher ones and some of the sailors from the Great Lakes Naval Training Center took it personally. Then George and the Riverview staff had them right where they wanted them. Those customers were bread and butter. Smoking mad, they would buy balls by the bucketful. Their aim did not improve with their temper and they wound up spending a ton of dough to just get that last dunk.

George and the other employees didn't mind getting dunked, especially when it was hot out. The little clerk had been right. This was a way to make some good money and have a few laughs at the same time. George just ignored the racial insults and foul mouthed behavior. That was their problem, not his. All George knew was that his good friend Rosa was coming over tonight and bringing ribs.

"Awright, toothpick, les'go. Maaan, how you gonna get that ball up here? Somebody give that sucker a hand!" Out came that now famous and familiar deep belly laugh: "Haw, haw haw, Yessiree, y'all can't lay a han' on me! Ho ho, ho."

It was 1950 now and there was a new war on. Some God-forsaken place over by Japan, some folks called it. Korea. George felt that this was just not so. To him there was no such thing as a God-forsaken place. His readings and the Bible itself taught him that God was everywhere. God did not leave anyplace or any person. What usually had happened was that the person, the sinner, moved away from God. George's faith and his reason told him that all things happened for a reason and for mankind's good. He liked to think that we were all, colored and white, Indians, Mexicans, and Asians, we were all God's children. We were put here to work together, help each other and to live in peace together. Why did something so simple and obvious to anyone with a grain of sense have to be so difficult to achieve?

George had been working at Riverview and the African Dip for some five seasons now. It was time to get into something different. After work he stopped in at the employment office to talk to the foreman. Both the little clerk and the burley old Polock were gone now. The new boss listened to George. His name was Goldman and he was Jewish but was very different from the old timers. Very gentle. Polite even. "You are absolutely correct, Mr. Duncan, it is time for you to move up to a real ride." George held his breath. Maybe things were looking up at the old amusement park.

"I think I have just the place for you." He smiled at George. "We have an opening in the Tunnel of Love. It's a great place to begin with ride operations and you can move up from there. You can make almost as much as you were and stay a lot drier. I think you've been dunked enough! Time for you to dry out and try something different."

They showed George the Tunnel of Love. Set in a park-like setting, it had quite a few trees around it and was really just a loop of channels with moving water. The current was running good and steady but this was not meant to be a scary ride. This one emphasized tranquility and the more the better. There was a covered roof over almost all the channels and the water, though cold, was not any deeper than 2-3 feet. The wooden boats were about 12-14 feet long with seats for about four couples. George's job was to maintain the boats, then release them so that each group had the feeling that they were the only people in the tunnel.

He came to love that job and was the perfect man for it. No more insults, slurs, or being wet all day and into the night. Now he could outdo Cupid himself. He always had a gracious, southern charm anyway, but now that was put to an even better use as he acted the host of gentility to one and all.

This is where we met George. The Tunnel of Love was one of our favorite spots. Not that we were interested in (ugh!) romance, but it allowed us to raise some funds to supplement our meager allowances and savings so we could get to the BOBS, the Silver Flash, the Fireball, the Shoot the Chutes water ride, and our favorite, the Pair-O-Chutes tower with real parachutes. On some rides you could go again for a cut rate, usually a nickel or two cents. So, if you had some spare change, you could keep up a pretty good cycle for a small amount of dough. Gayle Snyder Holly, my first crush from the old neighborhood, remembers riding the BOBS fifteen straight times with Danny Del Grosso, whose folks owned the Kickapoo Inn at 79th and Stony Island. I don't know about you, but after five times in a row, they would have had to carry me off that ride. Danny would have been a great guy to go on a date with. He was quite a football player at Our Lady of Peace and Mount Carmel—a strong lineman and a good guy. His Italian family had won the Irish Sweepstakes in one of those Only in America stories and so he probably could have set the Guiness Book of World records for consecutive rides on the BOBS if he had wanted to do so.

Our gig was to panhandle the sailors and young guys as they were getting on the boats at the tunnel and persuade them that if they would pay our way on we would make it worth their while. Once we got on, and sometimes we could talk George into a freebie, we would get about halfway through the tunnel, then jump out into the cool, dark, running water and hold the boat. There was never a complaint from any of the riders or their dates but along would come boat number two, and three, and so on. Finally after about fifteen minutes, George had no more boats and began shining his big flashlight into the tunnel and hollering at us. We would then either wade out of the tunnel or hop in the first boat and release the traffic jam. It was always a hoot to us and the riders all appreciated it, even giving us an extra tip now and then.

Funny thing. We got to know George very well even doing odd jobs like cleaning up the boats, or going to get pop or coffee for him. We knew that George was headed into something religious because he was always talking about it and all the books that he had read. He was a high up kind of Deacon in his church on the West side but he kept on working and saving, eventually marrying Rosa and opening up his own church at 800 South Spaulding, also on the West side. The Reverend George Washington Duncan had done alright for himself.

They called it the Tunnel of Love AME church and by all accounts it was a total success. Riverview Amusement park came to an end after the 1967 season due to a variety of reasons depending on who you ask, but it is all history now. However, anyone in Chicago, regardless of what neighborhood they came from, will never forget those wonderful two cent days and five cent nights where we could all “Laugh our troubles away at Riverview.” I wish we still could.

18

A CONVENTIONAL YEAR IN CHICAGO

1952 was a year of great change for us at Our Lady of Peace, a rite of passage year in many ways. Beverly Jean Magnuson wrote our class prophecy for the Chappel side eighth graders. The scene was the Lakefront Agricultural Fair of 1962. But by 1962, a once proud South Shore was fighting for its very existence. The old neighborhood had already changed drastically in racial composition and the blacks were pouring up from Mississippi and Alabama in droves. This put tremendous pressure on the old Black belt in Bronzeville, then on Woodlawn, then on South Shore. Crime and tensions were on the rise.

That was the real and ugly future. In 1952 we were certainly a sheltered lot. Geographically, we were more fixed than an Amish family. The Amish try to limit their social radius to ten miles through the horse and buggy. We did it through the CTA. My family, and we were far from alone in this, did not own a car. We would not get an automobile until 1954—my first year at DeLaSalle after a year at South Shore High School and a year in the Oblate Seminary at Carthage, Missouri.

Pat Hughes, aka Sister Jean Joseph, a wonderful Adrian Dominican nun now working in Chicago at St. Leonard's House and before that principal of Aquinas High School, did our class will and testament. Somehow, and this could not have been a unanimous selection, we willed to Father Friel "our best wishes for success in all his endeavors."

Father Friel was not universally loved. The rumor and reality was that money came before all things in this parish and certainly before social and athletic programs for the kids. Even the doors of the solid Romanesque church at 79th and Jeffery Boulevard were said to be painted by the U.S. Mint. I remember examining the doors carefully after hearing that and found it was true. The doors were dollar bill green and the paint even had minuscule multi-colored threads just like genuine U.S.-issued currency.

Ever since Father Ignatius McDermott, our own blessed Father Mac, left to do real missionary work with the winos and derelicts of Chicago's skid row on West Madison Street, the kids had taken a back seat in the parish priorities. In an odd way, some of us saw that as a blessing. It forced us to do for ourselves and that's just what we did. We organized our own baseball games, built our own diamonds and backstops in a 79th Street prairie. We set up our own games, umpired them and did a good job of scheduling them without any adult help.

In eighth grade we had a fair football team coached by OLP grads Bill Drew and Timmy McNamara, who were freshmen at Mount Carmel. All of this led to a certain amount of self-sufficiency and self confidence on our part. I cringe inside today when I see a group of kids involved in baseball, football or soccer surrounded by a horde of screaming parents. Adults should leave the kids alone and they'll all be just fine.

We willed our principal Sister DePorres our unsold candy bars, New World newspapers and unsigned pink slips so she could bequeath them to the next grade: Eddie Lyons, Jim Wall, John Coppe, Johnny Mack and company. We did give our eighth grade nun, old Sister Lucille, a "hearty thank you for her wonderful understanding which she has manifested many times during the year." Sister Lulu should have retired ten years before. A kind and gentle soul, she was clueless as to young adolescents with raging hormones. I spent the entire eighth grade year debating the flat-earth theory, wasting hours of time when any other nun would have pounded me into instant submission.

1952 was a pivotal period out in the real world. Pork Chop Hill was a raging battle in a far-off Korea. Queen Elizabeth was in her first year as the reigning Monarch of Great Britain and Northern Ireland. The Mau Mau were getting their dander up in Kenya. The French were fighting what they called The Dirty War in another far-off place called Indochina. Eva Peron was wasting away from a battle with cancer in Argentina.

At home, the KKK was on the march all through the South. General Eisenhower promised to go to Korea if elected president. Bob Mathias took the gold in the Olympic decathlon. The Yankees beat the Dodgers in a spectacular World Series. Rocky Marciano smashed, staggered and KO'd aging Jersey Joe Walcott to take the heavyweight championship and the Detroit Lions beat the Rams to win the NFL title before TV would change the game forever.

Closer to home in Chicago, we were feeling the impact of the steel strike that hit South Chicago and our own mills. Almost all of us had a friend, if not our dads, cousins or older brothers, who were directly affected by the strike.

Mount Carmel kept on rolling. 1952 would be their third championship season in a row. Junior Reynolds and "Buttsy" Pinn ran all over Abe Woodson and Austin High 27-14 at Soldier Field. South Shore and Our Lady of Peace were well represented on that team by Dick Prendergast, Bob Delaney, Bill Durham, Leon Dourlet and Danny Delgrosso.

Our real rite of passage as eighth grade graduates was being able to hitchhike downtown. Now that opened up our horizons. Most of us had been down to the Loop only with our parents or grandparents for special occasions, usually Christmas, Easter or to get our picture taken at the Koehne Studios.

I'm not sure if our jaunts were sanctioned but I don't think they were. We were naive but it was a different world then. We always left from the southeast corner of 79th and Jeffery. Across the street to the north was the OLP church and rectory. Kitty corner was Shapiro's Drug Store with Old Addie the crippled newslady out in front. Usually found in her dirty orange WWII flight coveralls and crutches, she was a neighborhood fixture. She had two sons, Bill and Joe, and both were bookies although I don't think Addie ever placed any bets herself. A Jewish woman, she had been paralyzed years before while rescuing a child from a certain car accident by throwing herself in the path of a speeding car. I think the kid was a gentile too. Probably Irish.

Somehow, we found out that both the Democratic and the Republican Conventions were being held in

Chicago that year. How Mayor Kennelly ever pulled that one off I'll never know. The conventions themselves were held at the old Chicago Amphitheater at 47th and Halsted, which was made famous by the histrionics of the 1968 Democratic Convention and is now gone forever.

We headed down to the place where the real power was brokered: the Conrad Hilton Hotel on Michigan Avenue across from Grant Park. Every day we would hitch a ride down to the Loop and I never had trouble of any kind. We did hear of one driver who made a suggestive remark to one of our buddies or maybe placed his hand on one kid's knee, but no one ever really bothered us at all.

At the Hilton we signed up to do volunteer work for different politicians. I got assigned to work for Sen. Richard B. Russell of Georgia (our motto was "Hustle for Russell"). We hustled alright. We rubbed shoulders with all the big shots of the day. You'd take a message up to Room 1245 and Vice President Albin Barkley would open the door. You'd take a platter of sandwiches up to 1837 and Senators Kerr and Estes Kefauver might be washing things down with some Jack Daniels, with a real coonskin hat hanging on the wall.

Delivering sandwiches was great. You'd leave with two dozen and come in with 18. Nobody minded and nobody kept count. Somehow we met a model named Darla. "Darla, da darling of da Dems" one wag called her. Darla was involved in a publicity stunt posing in a skimpy bathing suit wrapped in Russell banners on the fire escape in the back of the hotel on the Wabash Avenue side. Darla must have taken the "Hustle for Russell" motto seriously. She was up in room 1643 and we would run stuff up to her endlessly. Every time we got up there a different guy was answering the door.

She was blonde and gorgeous and always very friendly and kind to us kids, but it took us a long time to figure out what was going on. We were slow learners at the time.

We met everybody. Les Paul and Mary Ford, even Stepin Fetchit from the old flicks. We kept looking for President Truman but I'm not sure he was there because he had turned down the nomination on March 29th at a big Party dinner in Washington. I heard that he did fly in later on to support our own Adlai Stevenson. Stevenson was drafted in the first "genuine draft" of a presidential nominee in almost half a century.

The best thing anybody remembers about Adlai and that entire convention is the famous Life magazine photo of Adlai sitting and reading a Tribune with a hole in his shoe. Some people said it made him look like the absent-minded professor, a type of egghead who is clueless as to reality. I think he got some votes out of it though because it made him look more human. Heck, we all had holes in our shoes then anyway.

We saw Eleanor Roosevelt, "The First Lady of the World," but only from a distance. She reminded all of us kids of our grandmothers and we would have voted for her in a heartbeat if she would have run and we could have voted. We liked Henry Krajewski. Henry was the presidential candidate of the Poor Man's Party and that was our party of choice. He had a big rally out in Roseland at the Roseland Theater. A loudmouth, happy, portly man, he campaigned on a platform of "No Piggy Deals." He owned a pig farm in downstate Illinois. He even had a huge pig on a special leash that he would take for walks down 103rd Street .

My Uncle Al, who was a wonderful character that lived in Roseland near Roney's Real Rich Ice Cream factory, went to the rally because he heard there was going to be a supply of ham sandwiches. Also, Henry wanted to get us out of the UN and Korea and my Uncle Al was for that because he had a son fighting in those frozen mountains. Uncle Al probably voted for Eisenhower though because Ike had promised to go to Korea if he was elected. That was a little more realistic although Ike didn't have any ham sandwiches. Nobody knew what Ike was going to do in Korea once he got there but the fact that he would go there was enough for most people.

Funny story though and this is true. Ike came to Chicago after the Democrats left. He had taken a limo out to our old neighborhood in South Shore one night to see Murray "The Camel" Humphreys. It seems that Murray, who had taken over the Chicago syndicate after Capone died in 1947, held the key to the election with all kinds of union support that the mob was involved in. Murray had a so-called nondescript home at 77th and Bennett right behind our two flat and that is where Ike got the support that put him over the top. Well, politics makes strange bedfellows as they say. Although in Darla's case, I wouldn't call her a strange bedfellow. Everybody seemed to know her.

All of us got to know the Conrad Hilton Hotel very well from working those two conventions. For some reason, we spent much more time down at the Democratic Convention than the Republican one. Remember where we were coming from: the most Democratic city in the north. All of our city politics were Democratic. From Nick Bohling, our local alderman, to the lowliest sanitation engineer in the ward, everyone was, at least nominally, a Democrat.

Even after the conventions, we continued to enjoy our newfound sense of freedom and adventure. The big thing was to hitchhike down to the Hilton hotel after school or on weekends and then when it got dark, take the elevator up to the top floor and climb outside on the fire escape up to the roof. The ledge around the Hilton was as wide as a city sidewalk but we were about twenty-some floors up. Gravity being the enticer it is, we would start to heave things off onto Michigan Avenue. Little things at first, then bigger ones. I remember Bo standing on the ledge with a large wooden Adirondack chair over his head looking for all the world like Quasimodo. I believe cooler heads prevailed and the chair wound up back on the roof instead of on Balbo Drive in a thousand pieces.

A few years ago I saw a story in the Tribune. It said that two young kids were killed at the Conrad Hilton. They apparently had been goofing around up on the roof of the hotel when they hit an air shaft at night and took the fast one-way express down to the ground floor in about six seconds flat. It made me realize how close we must have been to disaster up on the same rooftop at night.

Somebody was really looking out for us! None of us ever got into politics although that would have made a good story. The closest I got was going to DeLaSalle High School at 35th and Wabash. That school was as politically connected as an institution could be. We have had four or five mayors, plus hundreds of lesser denizens in city offices, lawyers, judges and minor pols of all sorts.

My DLS buddy, Charlie Rotkis was well connected because he lived in Bridgeport and had real aldermanic connections. One summer he got a hack job giving out tickets to black folks in the projects who had unlicensed dogs.

I have heard that the life expectancy of a junior

officer in combat is rated in hours, if not minutes. I believe that a City Dog License Inspector's life expectancy in the projects was less than that. Without a weapon of any kind or any company or support or communication, he would cheerfully set out for the infamous Federal Street high-rise projects to make his quota. I am still not sure if he was just ignorant, cocky, tough, naive, brave, lucky or all of the above, but somehow he survived that hot, humid summer up and down the elevators if they were working, taking the stairs if they weren't, walking through the gangs, gangbangers, pimps, ho's, dopers, alkies, thieves and assorted never-do-wells. He had a city employee ID, a religious medal, a book of citations in triplicate and a pen. That was it. The only white guy in the building. I've known some tough cops in my time, straight and otherwise, and none of them would go into that dangerous area, even armed and in force, if they didn't have to.

Charlie did have an advantage though. He inherited some genetic sales material from his dad who was a crackerjack old line sales guy at the big Spiegel's store on 35th Street. His mom was a wonder of an Appalachian woman with great inner strength, a warm sense of humor and a gift of gab and storytelling that could enchant any would-be evildoer.

He would make his rounds like the old lamplighter, wandering up and down the dirty halls and stairwells listening for the sound of any dogs. This may sound a bit bigoted, but I think that his odor was inherently different than the average welfare bopper in those buildings. When he got close to an apartment with a dog or dogs in some cases, those dogs would go nuts! Howling, screaming, drooling, smashing against the doors and walls even, they were almost viciously insane. These were not poodles, cocker spaniels, and Chihuahuas either. These were no pedigree junk-yard dogs of the worst kind: Dobermans, German Shepherds, Pit bulls, Rottweilers, and mixed breeds of every canine DNA possible. They were literally the worst dogs in show! If the American Kennel Club would ever hold its annual show here in the ghetto, I suspect that none of the snooty handlers and their pampered puppies would ever survive to make the trip back east.

Didn't bother Charlie. Cool as a cucumber, he would knock politely on the splintering, shuddering door. KNOCK-KNOCK: "Uh, hello, do you have a dog in there? This is the city inspector and I need to see his license please." Two more times, three. Finally a disembodied voice: "Aw, maaan, I ain't got no dogs in here. Whassa matter witchu?"

"Come on sir, I think you've got a dog in there....Open up, please. This is the city inspector. I don't want to have to call the cops."

GROWWELL, SNARRRRRL, BAM, BANG, GROWWELLL. ARRGH!

"Sir, it sure sounds like a dog to me, open up right now."

Eventually the bolts would slide open and the door would grudgingly open a crack, at least to the safety chains, and the negotiations would continue. "Sir, has your dog had its shots?" Silence. "SIR? MA'AM?" "Shee-it, Mr. Honkie, This dog done been shot three times already. Now leave us alone, y'hear." Charlie was nothing if not persistent, though, and usually got his man—er, dog!

We were moving on into high school now and the grade school innocence was over. It was a whole new ballgame as they say, they were playing for real and our lives were going to be changed forever.

19

MOM AND "THE CAMEL"

"He was skinny and dapper and handsome in a sinister sort of way, a representative of the new breed of racketeer, part thug and part businessman. And he enjoyed Capone's favor."

- Capone: The Man and the Era, by Laurence Bergreen

Well, it's Mother's day again. I'm sure that Hallmark is happy, as are the florists of the nation and all the restaurant owners, but not the waitresses of course, since most of them are moms in their own right.

My mom died unseasonably and unreasonably young at only fifty-four, which seems incredible now. In fact, she lived only nine years after my next younger brother Donnie died in 1960. So more than any other time of the year, my thoughts go out to her on this special day.

She had her share and more of serious problems, which cannot be denied. Not the least of these problems was having to struggle with Donnie having both polio and muscular dystrophy. Whatever her faults, her unfailing Irish wit and good humor cannot ever be overlooked. It was probably the heart of her generosity and her resiliency.

Marie Hannan Lewis was always a people person of the first degree. She worked primarily in sales. Mostly small places really, bakeries and local shops. The one exception when she worked at the Continental Bank downtown in the Loop for a while. That was later of course. Most of the time while us kids were young she was at home like most other moms in South Shore in the late 40s and early 50s.

Of her working days, I remember her most in her last job. It was with Ace Hardware in South Chicago Heights. She took to that job like the proverbial duck to water. You'd have thought that she was a part owner or at least on some kind of stock dividend plan. She knew everybody, greeted everyone by name, and took care of you like you were a long lost son or daughter. The only other job I ever saw her as enthusiastic about, although she loved all of them, was when she worked for John F. Kennedy's presidential campaign in Chicago in 1960.

You would have thought she and Pierre Salinger were best buddies and that it was her campaign strategy that led to the victory. (Maybe it was!) There could have been no harder working campaign worker anywhere in the country. Enthusiastic and loyal to a fault. Dedicated. The writing and work she did for them was excellent and the results, we felt, spoke for themselves.

Upon her graduation from Aquinas Dominican High School at 72nd and Clyde Ave.in 1933, she was offered a Journalism scholarship at Valparaiso University. This was a classy proposition in the depths of the Great Depression. It could have made all the difference in her life in so many ways, but it was not to be.

My Grandfather, Joe Hannan, would have none of it. "No!" he stormed, (I can almost hear it now). "It's a waste of everybody's time and money!" He was adamant: "Women don't belong in college—they'll just waste the education because all they'll do is get married and have babies."

Well, Papa, things are different now. Would have been different for her too. For all of us for that matter because she was dating guys like Bob Johnson, who became president of the ICRR and Ed "Moose" Krause, star athlete from Aquinas and a later transfer to DeLaSalle. Later, Moose would become a legend at Notre Dame, first as a star all-round triple letterman, and then as athletic director for decades. I might have been Gerry Johnson or Gerry Krause.

But life is funny, as they say. So my mom-to-be married my dad, Don Lewis in 1934. But since he was an Episcopalian, they had to be married in the Our Lady of Peace rectory, on Jeffery Boulevard, not in the church itself. Documents had to be signed to ensure that all the children would be raised Catholic. Ah, the "good old days!" Authority forever!

My dad was working for the IC railroad as a conductor at the time, hence it was in their company hospital on Stony Island Avenue at 57th that I would be born on June 11, 1938. Later he would sign on with the old Mall Tool Company at 79th and Stony Island Avenue (at South Chicago Ave.). He would work on military production at Mall all through the war years, right up to and including the time 'Old Man' Mall moved his company out to Park Forest around 1955 even before the neighborhood changed.

When my Grandfather Hannan built his own home (all by himself) in Cedar Lake, Indiana in 1947 and 1948 and moved out to the country in 1949, we took over his first floor apartment at 7711 Constance. My great-uncle, Ed Hannan, and his wife Amy continued to live on the second floor.

It was like a new life to us, although the territory was not at all unfamiliar. Best of all, I did not have to change schools. I did not even have to change rooms at school. I could stay on the familiar Chappel side. I thought I had the best of all possible worlds.

We soon found out, however, that we had a very interesting neighbor. Across the alley from us at 7710 Bennett, lived Murray Humphreys. As in Murray "The Camel" Humphreys. As in Al Capone's right-hand man, Humphreys.

The crime encyclopedias say that he got the nickname from his penchant of wearing expensive camelhair coats. We knew better. It was just from his old nickname of the "Hump." All right, maybe it was both things together that made "The Camel" a natural.

The only non-Italian in the Chicago "Outfit," he invented the concept of laundering ill-gotten money through the acquisition of legitimate businesses. He could have been a great lawyer, and certainly had a keen mind by most accounts, but he operated outside the law his entire career. Funny thing, he was always open and honest about being a crook. There was never a pretense that he was anything else. He was proud of both his crookedness and his 'honesty'.

A strikingly handsome Welshman with curly black hair, he was always well dressed and groomed to the nines. He later became the prototype for the character of Tom Hagen, the only non-Italian in the Don Corleone "family" in The Godfather series. He was quiet and always appeared polite and unassuming.

There was no "hail fellow, well met" about him at all and he took no part in any of the neighborhood functions. It was a simple case of live and let live as far as we were concerned. We didn't bother him and he didn't bother us.

People seem surprised now that a top mobster would live in a regular neighborhood. You have to remember that crooks didn't want to live where they "crooked." Crooks wanted to live in good neighborhoods for the same reasons that all the rest of us wanted to live there: nice schools and churches, safe streets, and a good environment for their families and their children.

The Camel had only one daughter, Llewella, who went to South Shore High School at the time we moved into the neighborhood. She was lacking a date for the senior prom so her dad phoned out to California and called in some chips. Frank Sinatra was on the next plane to Chicago and took her to the dance. When she graduated from high school, she was given a graduation party like so many other kids. The only difference was that the entertainment at her party was Old Blue eyes himself: Mr. Frank Sinatra. All that stuff didn't impress me too much because I never cared for Sinatra, but I just tell you so you get an idea as to the tenor of the times and the background of the neighborhood.

Murray Humphreys' home was something else indeed.

The history books I've seen lately call it "non-descript" but it sure was "descript" to us. I was never inside it but the exterior was classic Mob. A beautiful Tudor style home without ostentation but it was as secure as a home could be. It was surrounded on three sides by a high, electrified fence secured in a low concrete wall. Double barbed-wire V's finished off the top. Sounds like a prison, but it really was rather discreet; at least he left off the guard towers.

In the back, directly across from our garage, was a unique arrangement consisting of a locked gate, next to which, in ascending order, was a large steel grocery box, topped by a steel-encased refrigerator, topped off by a steel-encased telephone. All the boxes were keyed in and keys were given only to selected and trusted vendors. After deliveries were made, the serviceman would call up to the house and a maid, butler, or bodyguard would promptly appear to bring in the delivered goods without having to open the gate.

One night in early December 1951, Northside nightclub owner Sam J. Rinella was gunned down and killed by two hoodlums in front of his beautiful blond wife at his home at 78th and Chappel, only few blocks east of our two flat. Who Sam was connected with and why the mob made the hit, I don't know and if I did know, I wouldn't tell. Rumor had it that some high ranking Chicago police officers were silent partners in the club. I can tell you it made a real "hit" in our neighborhood. Always has. Right to this day the case has never been solved.

A number of us kids had been in or around the area that night and all of us seem to have our own memories of portents and suspicious cars and side streets being mysteriously "blackened out". (My buddy Murph says he remembers shots that night, but then he always had an overactive imagination).

Sam's funeral was vintage gangland. A real classic. Limos, flowers, wailing and weeping. Women in black. Right out of The Sopranos! Our Lady of Peace was flowered as probably never before. Those of us who served the mass had a sense of being a part of history and the amount of the tip to the altar boys has grown over the years.

As you can imagine, the Camel was nervous now. Heck, we were all nervous. He then did what any reasonable and prudent man would do: he changed his daily routine. Instead of being picked up by his chauffeur in front of his house on Bennett, he and one or two bodyguards would come out the back, cross the alley, sneak through our narrow gangway, and get picked up in front of our two flat on Constance.

This was all workable for awhile except that he always seemed to come through with his entourage at the time my brother Donnie was waiting to be picked up by a special wheelchair bus. My mom was petrified. In her mind, all she could see was one of those classic scenes made famous by Hollywood where James Cagney and a black car full of tommy-gunners would spray a hail of lead into our aptly named gangway, taking out the Camel, his henchmen, and my little brother in his wheelchair. What a funeral mass that would have been!

My mom was definitely the easygoing type when it came to us kids, but when it came to her son's safety she could get her Hannan Irish up in a hurry! She made up her mind to confront the Camel the next time it happened and confront him she did. I kept trying to tell her not to do it. "Ma, no. Please don't do it!" "Ma, just leave him alone." But she wasn't going to listen to me.

It was a fine spring morning in 1952 as I remember. Donnie was out in front in his wheelchair and the gang came into our backyard. Mom was ready. Out the back door she came, "Good morning, Mr. Humphreys. Could I please have a word with you?" she called sweetly. I don't know if they had ever met before but the Camel could play the role of the most suave gentleman you ever saw.

He and the boys came to a halt in the back yard as the limo pulled up in front and my mom let him have it with both barrels, figuratively speaking, of course. She explained her fears that if something happened to him, my brother would certainly be injured or killed and, she pointed out, Donnie had suffered enough already. She would have melted even Al Capone's black heart, let alone the Camel, who acted as gracious as he could be.

Not appearing to take any offense at all, he assured my mom that everything would be OK. Smiling, he seemed to sense both her fears and her resolve immediately.

One thing for sure, he never used that pickup routine again. Off they went and we never ever saw them again in our yard. I think we went out for Chinese food that night on 79th Street—a sure sign of celebration usually reserved only for payday.

One odd thing though. About two weeks later an envelope showed up in our apartment building mailbox with a sizable cash donation for my brother's school. Mom took it to the next Gompers PTA board meeting where it was promptly and unceremoniously rejected. Thumbs down!

"Blood money!" they said. "We don't want that kind of donation." I never knew what happened to that envelope. However, now that I really think about it, I am sure it was just after that that we got our first TV. A big one! No more peeking through the neighbor's windows and reading lips.

Mom, you were nothing if not practical. Happy Mother's Day! Forever.

20

KOSHER SOUTH SHORE: AN IRISH TRIBUTE

To many of us at Our Lady of Peace, it seemed we were just another Chicago Southside Irish neighborhood, but in reality, we were an Irish/Jewish neighborhood. What an unlikely pair, but what a wonderful combination!

Bar Mitzvahs and Irish Wakes. Irish tap dancing and the Hava Nagila. The IRA and the Stern gang. Soda bread and Challah. Saints and Prophets. Rabbis and priests. Barney Ross and Packy McFarland. "No Irish need apply" and "No Jews allowed." The "Holy Ground" and the "Holy Land." Larry Cohen and the Neary brothers. Denny McLain and Sid Luckman. Guiness and Manischevitz. The House of David and the South Side Irish. Marshall Goldberg and Tom Carey. Tommy O'Connell and Marv Levy.

Somehow we all got along fairly well. I don't remember any overt anti-Semitism but maybe we were too young and naive then. People talk about the South

Shore Country Club not admitting Jews or Negroes and I remind them that they didn't admit any "Shanty Irish" like us either: Lace Curtain only!

The population of South Shore in 1940 was 79,595. Now that was a good sized town anywhere for those days, and even now. The 1940 census showed the largest number of foreign-born residents coming from Russia, Sweden and Germany, followed by the "Irish Free State," England and Wales. I don't know about the Swedes, but I suspect that many of the Russians and Germans were Russian and German Jews escaping from the war zones before the curtain came down for good.

Bob Levi (South Shore High School, 1954) described the neighborhood attitude best:

> "My folks raised me not to consider religion or ethnicity as a criteria for having friends. One of my best friends in high school and also college was Patrick Joseph Doody, Jr. Can you think of a more Irish-Catholic name? His dad had been raised Catholic, but his mom was Methodist. Rick had asked me to sing in the St. John's choir. Mrs. Doody always considered me her 'Jewish son.'"
>
> - Bob Levi, South Shore High School, 1954

My feeling is that the American Jews were wise not to build their own schools. It seems that they have had the best of public education and then added Hebrew school to teach Judaism. South Shore High School even had Hebrew in the curriculum as a foreign language. I always felt that it was the Jewish kids at South Shore High who added the real class to that school. They seemed to me to be intellectual, studious, and polite, yet had a wonderful, if slightly wacky, sense of humor and great resilience. It was usually the Protestants and most of the rowdy Irish-Catholics who were in trouble, goofing off, fighting, playing hooky, and generally going nowhere fast.

The Jewish kids had strong family ties. Not that the Irish and others didn't, but it was just not the same. It seemed that we had more than our fair share of broken homes, alcohol problems, gangs and juvenile delinquency. Bob Levi again:

"Just consider our high school class. Religion didn't matter and still doesn't. During high school years, we knew who the Jewish kids were and those who weren't. It really didn't matter with one exception. Most Jewish kids dated other Jewish kids. But I think that was probably true of the non-Jewish kids too."

- Bob Levi, South Shore High School, 1954

My take on it was that the Jewish kids were better off economically and had better clothes, more money and great opportunities. While the Jewish kids did better in their studies, the National Honor Society and Merit scholars and other scholarships, the Protestants and Catholics did better in athletics, particularly in football, baseball, basketball and track. Of course, there are always exceptions to any rule and some Jewish kids like Larry "Coco" Cohen and Shelly Stark rose to the top in south side basketball in the early to mid 50s.

My feeling was that it all had something to do with direction, goals and objectives. The Jewish kids seemed more focused on long range goals and were already thinking about college or university, a profession or business. We gentiles were more into the "here and now." Instant gratification, they call it today. We were focused on the present and allowed the future take care of itself. The other thing was that the Jewish kids had well defined boundaries while the rest of us were allowed to run much more freely.

The other angle to me was that the Jewish kids generally seemed to be living their faith in their daily lives while we Christians often seemed to compartmentalize our religion into Sundays versus the rest of the week—and they did not always match up.

My friend in Chicago, Jeff Heilbrun, (South Shore High School, 1962) who is almost singlehandedly rebuilding South Shore through an innovative urban renewal and rebuilding program that is revitalizing the old neighborhood and giving opportunities to young minority individuals and families, remembers:

"For a young Jew, the Catholic places were mysteries...we certainly did not have the level of communication about religions as is available today. We either learned through our parents or possibly a friend. Maybe starting with a Christmas mass to find our way in during a celebration."

- Jeff Heilbrun, South Shore High School, 1962

I would say that the Catholic places were a mystery to us too. Roman Catholicism is based upon a number of "mysteries" to begin with, and the service, at least in the old Latin Mass days, was very mystical, particularly at the High masses: loads of incense, bells, incantations and candles. My Irish buddies and I called it "the Magic Show."

I wish that we all could have had better communication and education about our respective religions. The prevailing viewpoint I recall was that interactions and an exchange of ideas with others was not only not encouraged but tantamount to a mortal sin. Visit a synagogue or a (gasp) Lutheran church? Goodbye Charlie! You were a goner. I hope that narrow viewpoint has vanished now.

Dr. Kiya Immergluck (South Shore High School, 1961) adds her personal perspective:

"I have quite a story about my encounter with a Catholic girl across the alley from me when I was 5 or 6 and she had to be 7 or 8. I'll never forget running into her in the alley one day when she came home in her strange plaid uniform. She must have had a big dose of propaganda that day, because she began picking on me because I was Jewish. I was totally shocked. She said things like, "You don't believe in our Lord, Baby Jesus!" Then she said that since Jesus was the son of God, that I must be praying to Joseph, Jesus's father. I stood up for myself and insisted that my God's name was definitely NOT Joseph, and she didn't know what she was talking about. I had great pride (even that young) that I was Jewish, and I wasn't going to let this girl push me around.

Here comes the strange part. I went home in an absolute rage. I decided that I hated ALL Christians and that they were all stupid for praying to that stupid baby Jesus! What happened next I always thought of as a miracle.

I cried myself to sleep, and had a strange and very real feeling dream. I was a little girl in a crowd of people crowded around a baby. All of a sudden, the crowd parted, and I saw Baby Jesus. He was beautiful and there was light radiating off his body. I fell to my knees and worshipped him.

I woke up the next morning totally free of prejudice against Christians. Many years later a born-again Christian badgered me for not immediately converting. I never did. To me, the miracle was that I was given a rare chance to see a completely different perspective and immediately heal my own anger and hurt."

- Dr. Kiya Immergluck, South Shore High School, 1961

This certainly shows the need for more personal interactions to teach interfaith tolerance and to appreciate our similarities as well as our differences. I remember being "adopted" by at least two Jewish families. One was by Jerry Levine and his wonderful family up the street from us at 75th and Constance. They became a real "storm home" for me in troubled times as a child as well as being a great home to visit anytime.

Carol Weiss from Hirsch High School and her fabulous and slightly wacky family, later became a real source of support and inspiration to me. They were warm, outgoing, loving, gentle people. Mrs. Weiss had a gig that was the closest thing to old time vaudeville. She billed herself as "the Queen of All Senior Citizens" (modesty was not her shortcoming). She was a good musician, singer and entertainer. I felt lucky to have known that special Jewish family as well as knowing Belle and Manny Lazar, who owned Wee Folks toy store up at 79th and Constance. That store was a real place of magic for all us kids, and the Lazars treated us warmly with good humor, respect, and all around good will. We loved that store and that family. Take a look at their daughter Caryn's book and website for a treasure trove of South Shore stories and reconnections: "The Pied Piper of South Shore". It is a loving tribute to Caryn's folks in the face of the tragedy when her father Manny, was killed in front of her mother during a robbery attempt in the new store on 79th Street in the early 1970s.

I don't think that the family or the neighborhood ever fully recovered from that terrible episode.

Sociologist Robert B. Smith from Bradwell, South Shore High School and Columbia University has another perspective for the years between 1949 and 1954:

"Interactions with Catholic kids were friendly among those in the same neighborhood, but marked by occasional physical conflict between outsiders and Jewish kids in the neighborhood. The "Brotherhood of the Bush" would occasionally enter South Shore, walking down Essex Avenue from 83rd to 75th Street to a bowling alley on the second floor at 75th and Essex. Several Jewish kids were severely beaten up. I was walking my dog and ran into this bunch but was not hurt badly; they liked my dog.

A year or two later we would congregate at 79th and Essex and the large numbers of girls and boys deterred such attacks. Occasionally, Mount Carmel kids might pick fights around 71st and Jeffery, but the damage was slight.

I might add that Mount Carmel kids living in our neighborhood were friendly and played basketball with us in the empty lots at 76th and Phillips, as did the O'Connell brothers who lived around 76th and Kingston. Those Irish kids went to South Shore and were famous for their athletic skills."

- Robert B. Smith, South Shore High School, 1949-1954

One Jewish man of honor from South Shore that I was personally privileged to know when I was teaching at Bloom High School in the late 60s was Leo Kushner. Leo owned the Paris Laundry around the post office at 75th and Paxton. He moved his business out to Chicago Heights in the early 1960s and I placed a number of handicapped kids at his business for job training. What a delightful man! He was a gentleman in every sense of the word. Visiting at his cleaners in Bloom Pla-

Plaza across from the high school became a special event for me ("Wednesdays with Leo") and we became good friends. Our main topics were South Shore and the Chicago sports scene. I probably spent more time on those job visits than I should have.

I still remember the rabbi at Leo's funeral at the temple in Olympia Fields telling us that Leo did not die of a bad heart. "Leo," he said, "was ALL heart!" He was right. Leo was one of the most gentle and generous men I have ever known. He not only took care of his family but he took care of his minority laundry workers like they were family too. I still feel as though Leo Kushner was one of the "Just Men" of Jewish folklore. May God bless his memory.

Another Jewish friend from my Bloom days is Dr. Jerry Coates. I worked with Jerry at Bloom when he was a school psychologist and I was working with the special education department. He was one unique individual. He had, like my younger brother Donnie, contracted polio as a young boy and wore long-leg braces. Whatever business his folks were in, they had prospered and they enrolled him early on at the Lab School at the University of Chicago, and he just kept on going, and going, and going.

He went all the way to a doctorate, very far indeed. However as far as some common day-to-day things, he just seemed to be out of it. I got the feeling that his mother was the stereotypical protective Jewish mom. If chicken soup could have cured polio, Jerry would have been in the Olympics and the Coates family even wealthier than they were.

He came over to our house from time to time for supper and Peggy asked him once if he would like some Oreo cookies with his dessert. "Oreo cookies, what are they?" he asked in surprise. He wasn't kidding. That was just one small example. Sports also were nil. White Sox, Cubs, the Cardinals, Bears, Blackhawks, or Bulls, it made no difference. He did not have a clue.

I don't know how we ever got along so well but we did. I guess he was my project in urban survival. He was great to work with, being so bright, good natured and generous to a fault.

Fast forward a year or so and Jerry somehow got a job as the first pyschologist in eastern Kentucky. He went to work for the John L. Lewis Mental Health Center in Prestonsburg, Kentucky. He was serving a multi-county area around Pike, Martin, Magoffin, and Hazard Counties. One place poorer than the next.

He rented a cabin in Pikeville and set about doing Appalachian social work/psychology operations in the heart of moonshine country. Every chance I got, I went down there to check up on this mind-boggling setup, usually during my spring breaks. It was an experience for me as well as Jerry. If you want to read a great account of the history of that area, pick up a copy of "Night Comes to the Cumberlands" by Harry Caudill.

Fast forward again. A few years later Peggy and I were at home one weekend in Matteson, Illinois and we got a phone call from Jerry asking if would be OK for him to stop by and introduce his new bride to be. To my knowledge, he had never had a date in his life and I was in shock. Sure enough, about ten minutes later Jerry shows up on our doorstep with his fiancé. Talk about being in shock. She was petrified. Turns out she had a third grade education and was working in the local five and dime. She had never been out of the mountains, never seen an elevator or an escalator. She was literally speechless. They had supper with us and she never said a word until our cat came out and hopped up in her lap. Then she opened up a little bit but not much.

We were invited to their wedding, which was the next weekend in the gorgeous Gold Coast apartment of Jerry's relative Ira Bach, overlooking Lake Michigan on Lake Shore Drive. I don't think that I have ever seen more of a mismatch culturally, educationally, religiously or any other way that I can think of. It was a beautiful wedding though and that was the last time we saw Jerry Coates or his bride. We wished them well of course, and who knows, maybe things went just fine. Jerry was headed to a new job at a Big Ten university as a faculty member there. Maybe it became a real Pygmalion story and she now has her doctorate in cultural anthropology and is on the faculty somewhere. At various times in the 70s and 80s I tried to look Jerry up but to no avail. So, if you find him before I do, tell him I'd like to see him again. I'd sure like to know the rest of the story.

By far the most powerful and emotional contact with the Chicago Jewish community for me was on a beautiful fall day in downtown Chicago. Peggy and I and our two daughters, Meg and Pam, were in the Loop. Peggy and the girls wanted to visit the Art Institute but it was such lovely weather, warm in the sun and cool in the shade and not too breezy, that I thought I'd leave them there and meander down Michigan Avenue. I didn't get too far though when I came to a crowd lining up on the sidewalk in front of the Spertus College of Judaica.

One thing I learned while growing up in Chicago is if there is a line, get in it. You never know what might be at the other end but it might not be all that bad. My old OLP buddy, John 'Bo' Bouhan did that one time on the near north side and wound up working for UPS and parlaying that chance opportunity into becoming one of the so-called "twelve disciples of UPS": a district manager with an early retirement and beaucoup bucks to boot. That is what Brown can do for you if you hustle and play your cards right.

Today though, this line was for something else. "A great man is coming today," someone said "A wonderful speaker who was a survivor of three Nazi concentration camps and who escaped from a Dachau-bound train in 1945 from an almost certain death." I had been by Spertus College many times before but had never gone in. Today for some reason I decided to go in and listen.

The speaker was an older gentleman with a mane of snow white hair who reminded me of David Ben-Gurion. I was struck by his rather matter of fact approach, as if he were relating a long ago camping trip story. He was not overly emotional and that made his message even more powerful and chilling to me. The auditorium was full. It was an older crowd, as you might expect. There was a host of blue haired ladies and balding older men. I suspect that many were survivors in their own right.

The speaker's name was Arnost Lustig and he was a Jewish Czech author who had written an account of his escape, survival and journey to the U.S. after the war. His book was titled Diamonds in the Night and he used the metaphor of the stars to represent the awful number of children killed in the Holocaust.

He said to us that as smug and comfortable as we were this beautiful fall day, that if we were locked in this auditorium together without food or water, it would not take but a few days and we would lose our veneer of civilization and become like beasts to survive. I saw folks looking sideways a little nervously at their neighbors.

He related his own experiences where fathers had been forced to fight to the death with their sons for the amusement of the Nazi guards. They were promised life if they acquiesced, but that promise was as hollow as all the others and they were themselves killed.

Arnost told us that he had seen great role reversals, unexpected and almost unexplainable. Rabbis stealing crusts of bread from women, children or the sick and dying. Criminals giving up meager rations so that mothers could feed themselves and their children one more day. Everything was turned upside down. Insanity reigned.

Then Arnost said something that I have never forgotten. He said that whenever he met a person today something inside him would ask "What kind of person would this person be if we were together in a camp today? What would they be like? What would they do?" It was a chilling thought and all of us thought about it long and hard.

All I know is that I usually have something to say to a speaker after a lecture but this time I did not go up to talk to him. I think I did not want to take the chance that he might shout out at me, "Yes, YOU. You who think you are so superior now. You would have been one of them! I know it."

I left to get back to the Art Institute and my family. They will probably never know why I hugged them so closely when I got them around me again, or why there were still a few tears in my eyes.

Last summer I had an opportunity to attend week-long Jewish conference at University of Wisconsin-Madison. It was a wonderful and intellectual time that I will long remember. All the conferees, except me, were Jewish and I did not realize how many kinds and types of Jews there are. Obviously there are the big three: Reform, Conservative and the Orthodox. I know that this is not all. Each of the three groups appear to have subgroups of their own. The only thing that I can relate it to are the Christian groups and subgroups; Catholics, Protestants, and shades of denominations in between from Unitarians to Mormons and Jehovah's Witnesses and the "wackos" from Waco.

The overall theme of the conference was Israel as she approached her Diamond Jubilee and the relationship of the United States to Israel. We looked at the relationship of the Judaic tradition in Israel where there is a kind of mandatory theocracy, versus the unique Judaic tradition and culture of the Jews in the New World. Here they are in a country that is based upon separation of church and state and where Judaism is a voluntary kind of "cafeteria style" religious experience.

This is not greatly different from the current struggle within the Catholic Church. The American Catholics are somewhat analogous to the Reformed Jews and I am sure that the Pope and the European Catholics look upon the American church as a lot of yahoos who just pick and choose what they want to practice.

It certainly leads to some lively debates and politics within both the Jewish and Christian community. What I did pick up at the conference was the concern of a number of speakers as to the loss of support from the American liberals as the Israel Defense Forces have been acting much more unilaterally and hawkish toward the Palestinians and other Arabs. A number of speakers expressed the fear that the Israelis are losing the "moral high ground" that they so clearly had during the 1948 War of Independence.

Professor Gil Troy from McGill University said in a recent article in the Jerusalem Post:

"Obligatory Judaism (in Israel) is like a command economy, guaranteeing high levels of participation, communal unity, and conformity, but risking low levels of creativity and satisfaction. Voluntary Judaism (in America) is like a market economy, risking more chaos, deviation and alienation but frequently yielding greater originality and individual fulfillment. Judaism is fundamental to many Israelis: they cannot imagine their lives without God, and most Israelis would feel smothered if somehow prevented from, say, ever speaking Hebrew again. For many American Jews, Judaism is utilitarian, a pleasant addition to their lives but one of many identities, ideologies, and hobbies they juggle. This dizzying choice in a vast spiritual and ideological supermarket explains those alarmist surveys reporting growing numbers of American Jews saying they would not consider Israel's demise a personal tragedy. They are being honest. Americans live in a disposable culture—a recent Pew poll reported that more than 40 percent of American adults have changed faiths since childhood."

- Professor Gil Troy, McGill University

Well, I have to admit that I am one of those 40 percent, having changed my faith since childhood but continuing to work less on doctrines and hopefully more on actions.

However, even I would feel that were Israel destroyed, it would be a personal tragedy. I am glad I went to the conference and would go again. I did not feel in any way separated, or trivialized but then again I was glad I was not required to wear an armband with a yellow cross on it.

I have the greatest respect for the Jewish culture in its many rich forms. I wish someday to see a lasting solution to the current tinderbox in the Middle East. Let's put it this way. If the Irish and British can find enough common ground to resolve their differences and live in peace, there is hope for anyone anywhere.

I feel that the Jews and other minorities have added a positive dimension to our national fabric. They are a strong and resilient people above all and they have a sometimes quirky but strong sense of humor that has sustained them through many trials and tribulations. I think Kiya Immergluck said it best:

"It's funny how certain incidents stand out in your mind. A girl must have heard that I was Jewish shortly after I arrived at my dorm at the University of Illinois in 1961. She came right up in my face and shouted, "You killed Christ!" I have always had a quirky sense of humor, so without the slightest hesitation, I said with a straight face, "I did NOT--it was my cousin Herbie!" She literally fell on the floor laughing, and we were fast friends after that!'"

- Kiya Immergluck

Now I am not saying that the Jews in America or old South Shore were perfect. Some stereotypes are true and they could sometimes be rude, loud and obnoxious (so could the Irish). But, taken as a whole, the Jewish community in South Shore was such an asset that any of their foibles can easily be overlooked and forgiven.

For my part though, I am glad that we were together in the old neighborhood and I feel that we can continue to bring a little bit of that wonderful sense of time and place to wherever we now call home. Shalom.

21

MICK'S STORY

My old Our Lady of Peace buddy Michael Barth,(Mick to us then but Mike now) stopped at the house recently for a pit stop and breakfast. I had just found his new address and had sent him a reconnection note. To my surprise, he called on a Friday night and told me that he would be leaving for his cottage in Iron Mountain, Michigan at 3:00 Saturday morning. He wanted to take us out for breakfast but we felt that we all would do better if he could just come on by for some home cooking.

Peggy put on waffles, scrambled eggs and ham, coffee and grapefruit and we had a great visit. Mick was in fine fettle as usual and looked great! I think he could play a double header with Ernie Banks and go five for seven, with two walks. Mick did not look any older than he did the last time that we all got together (Phil Jordan, Pat, Peggy, and the Murphs at the Holiday Inn in Harvey in the 1980s).

I felt that he was genuinely interested in the nostalgia project, or whatever it is that we're doing. He had much to talk about and had a ton of details that I'd forgotten. He remembered that our seventh grade nun, Sister Ann's, name for the place to send miscreants in the back of the room was "nigger-heaven!" Very politically incorrect now, and bad manners at any time. Does that ring a bell with you? Did she really say that?

He sure remembered Super Don's 7th grade encounter with Sister Ann at OLP and the multiplication of fractions. Don's headprint is still in that blackboard! The only hit worse than that for Don was the plane crash he had in Florida while serving as a jumpmaster for the South Florida Parachute Club. He smashed the side of his face against the dashboard of a Cessna and broke every major bone in his body.

Mick talked about things from the old days and OLP. He was glad to hear that I had been in contact with Father Mac the day before. He remembered Father Mac with great respect, admiration, and fondness. He talked about the conflicts that Father Mac had with His Royal Majesty Friel about the basketball courts going in on the playground. It seems that HRM wanted the courts taken out because of the possible damage to his beautiful Cadillac.(the "Monsignormobile"). Father Mac went to bat for the kids as always but I am not sure what the outcome was, although I can guess. It reminded me of a real "Mr. Roberts" kind of situation. This may have eventually led to Father Mac's transfer to Catholic Charities downtown at 126 North Des Plaines.

Mick's current passion is golf. Makes a lot sense. I've always felt that Mick was the best natural athlete in our school days. He was offered a semi-pro baseball contract but his dad vetoed that idea: "Are you crazy?

Throw away your future for a lousy twenty-five bucks a game! Sleep in flophouses and ride on broke down buses! For what? To waste your future? You're going on to school and then take over our laundry business. You'll never go wrong with La France laundry!"

Old Man Barth was a great guy in many ways, but professional sports did not represent the future to him. Too bad we weren't born about forty years later. Mick would be playing for the Cubs, making $1.5 million per year and batting .240 or better. No, the future was work and that work was going to be in the La France Laundry on 75th Street in South Shore.

It's too bad that Mick wasn't born into my family in one way. My dad was a semi-pro baseball player and played in the southern leagues during the early 1930s until the inevitable caught up with him: then it was work on the IC railroad, and W.W. Grainger and finally to work for another German dictator: "Old Man" Mall, owner of Mall Tool Company at 79th and South Chicago Ave.. I know my dad would've given a lot to have had a son with the innate natural ability that Mick had.

Coming out of Marietta, Ohio in the depths of the Depression, Mr. Barth got ahead the hard way. Moving to Chicago, he took on some of the toughest work the South Chicago steel mills had to offer. He was always a feisty little bulldog of a man with a sense of Germanic authority. In any event, ball playing was not viewed as a viable option by members of that generation.

Mick's dad was no slouch. He had sixteen-inch forearms from pulling slag on overtime shifts in the mills. He wanted to leave his sons a legacy greater than going to work in the mills and coming out forty or fifty years later with broken health and a cheap retirement watch. So Mick went to work at La France laundry at 2141 East 75th Street. Brother Tommy went there too. Paul,

Paul, the baby of the family, probably would have wound up there as well, if he hadn't been killed in a tragic auto accident in 1981.

Mick was the hardest working kid that I ever knew. After school, Saturdays, summers, vacations, it didn't matter. The only days Mick and the boys ever had off were Sundays and holy days. They worked long hours too.

Opposites attract, they say. With the Barths it would seem that way. Mick talks about the hard side and the soft side of his and his family's personas. The hard side was that German authority. The soft side was represented by his wonderful mother's Bay City, Michigan Irish clans of the Connollys and the O'Hanleys. Male, female, German and Irish; We sure had complicated sides in our makeup.

Old Man Barth could not bring himself to say "I love you" to any of his sons. Mick conned him into it one day in a scene reminiscent of the old "I love you Dad..." "You're not going to get my Bud Light!" commercials. The old man would finally say, "So do I" to Mick after

Mick would tell him that he loved him. Mick slipped in a "so do I" before his dad could and his dad said, finally, "I do love you!"

Mick's mom was a peach. Gentle, loving to a fault, even though crippled up and racked with severe rheumatoid arthritis, she was always gracious and generous to us kids. She was a close friend of my mom's mother, Mrs. Rowena Hannan. The Hannans had bought a two-flat at 7711 Constance Avenue around 1926 in the great South Shore building boom before the Depression. The Barths at that time were living close by at 78th and Euclid. This proximity, coupled with a deep Catholic devotion that both women had to Our Lady of Peace parish, led to a lifelong friendship.

With my grandfather Hannan's talent in plumbing, electrical work and construction, I would not be surprised to find that he had done some work at La France laundry. My grandfather, Joe Hannan, was a true jack of all trades. His shop was on Stony Island Avenue between 67th and 68th Streets and he did free work for Aquinas High School when my mom and aunt were going there. He eventually built his own home out in Indiana in the Cedar Lake/Crown Point area when he was in his 60s and maintained an electrical motor repair shop out of that home until his death in 1960. Both my grandparents died that year and are buried at Holy Name Church in Cook, Indiana just west of Cedar Lake.

The house that I will always remember the Barth family connected to is 8223 Oglesby Avenue. 82nd and Oglesby was a little beyond my territory from 77th and Constance. Had we stayed at 79th and Phillips, things might have been different, but as it was I hung around more with the older guys, Jack Sheehan, Bob Smith, Fran Melaniphy, Gary Williams, and Mike Hughes and company from the Jeffery side after we moved to the apartment on Constance.

One place that Mick and I both connected on was Moline's. Mo's, as it was popularly called, was the OLP school hangout at 79th and Jeffery, although the Tastee Freeze and Pla-Mor Lanes gave Mo's a run for its money. Its claim to fame was the greasiest hamburgers ever known. Fifteen cents each and if the Molines (Mom, Pop and son Ken) had played their cards right, the double arches and the sign with "Millions and millions sold!" would stand for Molines instead of McDonalds. Mo's was a great place for a snack, to meet the guys, "hubba-hubba" the girls, lag pennies, or line up a game of alley basketball at Grannon's. Or just talk. Or just shut up and listen.

Mick got to know 79th Street pretty good. Going to Leo High School at 79th and Sangamon meant taking the 79th Street bus west to school. Almost the entire neighborhood went to either Leo or to Mount Carmel. Best rivalry in the city. The Leo class of '56 was a good class with a lot of OLP kids: Jim Sherman, Terry Tobin, John Gleiter, Harry Gerrity, Joe Bieber, Ralph Gatto, Don DeLa Mar, and of course, Mick. The 50th reunion is over now but who's counting? Mick was accepted at Notre Dame and now regrets not going. He did get two years in at Loyola on a La France Laundry scholarship: working and commuting. He still wants to finish up and, if I were a betting man, I'd bet on Mick in the financial field: securities, stocks, bonds and commodities. Then retirement and golf.

Mick married Carol early. Too early. That marriage did not last. He was always more mature than the rest of us. It had a lot to do with a solid work ethic and a real family business always in need of attention. He had four children: Michael, Colleen, Noelle and Greg. Colleen is in Maui, Hawaii and has been the athlete of the family excelling in track, volleyball and other sports, even going for an Olympic tryout at one time.

Michael Jr. is dead. He died December 18, 1994. Losing a brother is tragic, of course, but losing a child has to be bitter indeed. Mick is coping with this with a strong sense of resiliency. I feel that he has had a good deal of support from and through his family and his strong foundation of religion hasn't let him down. Neither has his second wife, Pat.

Resiliency has been a key word for many of us from OLP. We were Depression babies raised in wartime. We did a lot for ourselves because we had to. No Little League. We organized things on our own.

No organized playground activities—we did it ourselves. No prosperity, at least until the 1950s. No dating services. No unemployment compensation—just do it on your own. Of course we were helped by our families as we help our own now. However there was a strong Eisenhower sense of quiet self-sufficiency that has helped us survive life's ups and downs.

Mick's younger son Greg is in California. He graduated from California Polytechnic State at San Luis Obispo.

I got a sense from Mick that his second wife Pat, has been a solid mainstay through many joys and tribulations. They have a son, Scott, who is currently living up in Iron Mountain, Michigan. Scotty and Beth have one child and one coming. These grandchildren are the pride of the present and the hope for the future for Mick and Pat, and in a sense, for all of us.

Pat is a registered nurse and has worked her way up the old fashioned way: she's earned it! Leaving Bremen Township High School early to help support her family, she has continually worked her way up the nursing and the professional ladder. She recently received her bachelor's degree and is working on master's.

Mick's dad is gone now like most of our parents. He was a great influence on our classmate Don DeLaMar. He certainly influenced Super Don in the area of aviation, being a long time private pilot himself. He was an avid sportsman and hunter who raised pheasants in Michigan and flew cross-country on hunting trips when the only people who could do that were movie stars and millionaires. Now we see Don doing the same thing!

Mick, we wish you well. You have always been a delight to be around with that crazy cackle of a laugh that we appreciated so much. You do have a soft side but you can take care of yourself if need be. Stay well, keep out of sand traps on the course and in life. Keep on learning. Finish your degree. Keep smiling. Stop on by.

22

CHICAGO: THE CITY THAT WORKS!

"Sha na na na, sha na na na na,
Yip yip yip yip yip yip yip yip
Mum mum mum mum mum mum
Get a job Sha na na na, sha na na na na
Every morning about this time
she get me out of my bed
a-crying get a job."

- Get a Job, The Silhouettes

Labor Day is always an appropriate time to look back at those beginning jobs we had as kids. They were the building blocks, or should we say the Tinker Toys, of where we are in our vocations today.

Chicago was and is a great place to work. It's an endless assembly line of jobs, places to work and things to do. No matter where you are working today, be it for the city as a fireman, cop or ward heeler, whether you are a lawyer, educator, have your own business, or you are in the religious arena, whether you are a housewife, hooker or in another entertainment arena, you didn't begin there.

You had to begin someplace else. On the South Side you started out in the neighborhood at the most menial of jobs, gradually working your way up the slippery ladder of success. The great thing about Chicago was the infinite variety and sheer numbers of opportunities that it offered. If a job didn't pan out for one reason or another, you only had to wait a little while for the opportunity train that was usually pulling in just after the other one pulled out.

My first job, a regular paid job with a timesheet and all, was washing and cleaning cars in 1949 for the Island Auto Sales at 7953 Stony Island Avenue. Big Al Liss and his rancid cigar burned indelible memories into my young consciousness. Thirty-five cents an hour and not bad work when the weather was decent. I wish I had some of those collector's items now: 1940s Hudsons, Fords, Packards, even Studebakers. On my walk the other night I came across a yellow 1949 Kaiser convertible in mint condition. I wanted to get out my old bucket and chamois and give it a spiff right there. Old habits die hard.

Al Liss and his buddy Erv Pryzinski also ran the Southfield News Agency at 7949 Stony Island Avenue right next to Lagen's Recreation Center, which was a euphemism for bowling alley and pool hall. That was where most of our hard earned dough wound up. Lagen's was just behind both the Kickapoo Inn and the Avalon Theater, and much of our earnings went to support both of those establishments as well.

We labored long, hard and early getting out the Chicago Sun, Herald-American, Tribune (morning), the Daily News in the afternoon until it went under, plus a collection of oddball little specialty papers like the Southtown Economist, the South Chicago News, the Jewish Journal and even the Yiddish Abendpost. Ironically, our push carts-wooden splintered with great rumbly iron wheels reminded me of the carts you see in the Warsaw ghetto newsreels: piled high with possessions or bodies.

After a series of what I felt were rip-offs on Al's part, I parted company with the Island Auto Sales in a fit of temper that probably did neither of us any good. My dad must've helped me get my next job because he used to work for the same guy, Pete the Greek, who had a small grocery store at 79th and Bennett across from the Crane Brothers Pharmacy. I think it was at 1911 East 79th Street and was called the Jeffery Food Store. This was odd because Jeffery Boulevard was still over a block away. Maybe Pete thought Jeffery Boulevard had better name recognition than Bennett Avenue.

In any event, my dad, Don Lewis, had worked for Pete in the late '20s when Dad was going to Bowen High School. I believe that I rode the same crazy bicycle that my dad did because there was no way anybody as cheap as old Pete would have replaced it. It was an antique: cumbersome and clumsy, black with some faded advertising on both sides of the bar that separated girl bikes from boy bikes. The most distinctive feature was the gigantic, battered wire basket over the small front wheel. I suppose it was engineered correctly, but when fully loaded was a devil to maneuver in city streets and heavy traffic.

I did it all. I selected orders, packaged things, cut meat, swept up, cleaned up, stocked up, delivered groceries, washed windows, and whatever else needed to be done. The tips were not bad, the pay being about 50 cents an hour, although biking in the winter when the streets were ice-covered and treacherous made for some awfully hairy moments.

Jobs then seemed to come in a crazy-quilt pattern. Some were concurrent. We did everything imaginable. A favorite was always carrying groceries. Murph and I did this even earlier than the car lot job in '46, '47, and '48. We would just stop by Kroger or Jewel on the way home from school and solicit little old Jewish ladies or whoever else might want to have their groceries carried home. Invariably they lived blocks away and always on the third floor of a three-floor walkup. Hey, we had to start someplace.

The Murphys had a number of Jewish tenants and neighbors over at 79th and Yates. When I lived behind him over there from 1944 to 1949, we would often make a few shekels by turning on lights and the oven or doing shopping for some of those folks. I'm not sure we understood their religious rules, but it was a real blessing to be able to make a little money for candy, White Castle, or for the local Saturday movie thriller.

Probably the biggest summer job in our later grade school days was caddying over at the South Shore Country Club at 71st and South Shore Drive. Now it has been revived as the Chicago Cultural Center after being sold to the Chicago Park District. The new paint job is pathetic, however: an ugly brown shade instead of the shining white we remembered.

The country club was a gorgeous palatial mansion of a place with its own beachfront on Lake Michigan. The driveway entrance off 71st Street and Exchange was through a massive roofed gatehouse. All the walls were white or light cream. The grounds, of course, were immaculately manicured. It was a little piece of heaven on the lake and caddying was about as close as any of us were going to get to that part of the world of the Irish Mafia.

Our neighbors from 79th and Phillips Avenue, the Coughlans, had a grandmother living at the country club in one of the apartments. Our big treat at Christmas time was to be invited to the annual Christmas party. It reminded me of the Colleen Moore dollhouse at the Museum of Science and Industry: all crystal chandeliers, silver settings, velvet curtains, and solid mahogany furniture. We thought we'd died and gone to heaven when the elaborate Christmas decorations were added to the already sumptuous setting on the shores of Lake Michigan.

Caddying, however, was a rude awakening for us. It introduced us to a whole world of cronyism, bullying and snobbery. The caddy boss was a sneaky, skinny Polack named Squeaky. "Squeaky the Polack." We just assumed that was his real name but obviously, he must have had a real Polish last name. We were just never introduced to him on a formal basis.

On an informal basis he and his big fat Mexican buddy, Pancho, ran things with an iron hand, or fist. If you wanted to get out early or even get out at all, the proper payoffs or obeisance had to be made. Sometimes it was paid in cash or a share of your tips, candy, sporting goods, clothes—something usually had to be arranged to reserve or preserve your place in line. Even then there was no guarantee that you weren't going to work your way to the front and be ready to go when Squeaky would butt in with his late arriving buddies from the "Bush," the area around the steel mills, and you would be moving backwards instead of forward.

Even when you did get out on the course, you were not out of the woods, so to speak. Cheapskate golfers, bad tempered old men, hot humid days and lost balls all conspired to make me dislike golf, and most golfers, to this day.

We kids worked at both the Republican and Democratic conventions in 1952, the year we graduated from Our Lady of Peace. We set pins at the Pla-Mor Bowling Alley on 79th Street, the Stars and Strikes on 75th, and Lagen's on South Chicago Avenue.

We graduated to a mobile truck route, delivering cardboard boxes of groceries for one of the 'big' guys, on both 79th and 75th streets all through South Shore but usually more near the lake in Windsor Park and Cheltenham. It was grueling work, usually in the hottest or coldest or wettest weather. We found ourselves running up and down endless third floor walkups. It was a great way to keep in shape for football, baseball and handball. Who needed a wimpy YMCA?

We also worked at the Tastee-Freeze on the corner of 79th and Jeffery, the closest thing to a fast food joint that existed at the time. Another great job was delivering pizza for Locasio's Restaurant at 2660 East 75th. I wish I still had the 1953 Chevy we used to use.

We still delivered papers but only if absolutely necessary. The real fun job by that point was going out to the AAA Auto Auction in Dyer, Indiana and driving nearly new or used cars back into the city. The fact that we didn't have driver's licenses didn't bother us and apparently didn't bother the dealers either, since they had to have a way to get their cars back to the city.

We were paid $5.00 for the trip plus a token for bus fare to get from the dealership back home. On the way of course, we had to take a swing by Dor-Ellens on 76th and Coles or Moline's at 79th and Jeffery or by a girlfriend's house in the hope that she and some of her friends might be sitting outside as we tooled by in a late-model Cadillac, Packard or Buick.

Eventually, we graduated to Andy Frain ushering, which got us into all the big events free and paid fairly well besides. We worked at old Comiskey Park, Wrigley Field, the Chicago Stadium, and Soldier Field. We also worked for the Consolidated Concessions Company, cooking and selling hot dogs, hamburgers and peanuts at all the sports venues.

Back in the old neighborhood we worked summers at Sundstrom Steel at 8030 South Chicago Avenue. Old man Sundstrom was a real head case to work for but the pay wasn't bad for those days. We also put in our time at Solo Paper Box Company on 75th Street.

Charlie Warfield's aunt got us jobs in high school unloading mail at Union Station every Christmas. It was cold, rough and hard work but the dough came in handy for presents and parties. We worked in the steel mills in South Chicago during the summer, also did tuck pointing with Fast Eddie McCormick, worked construction, and in short, hustled all over the South Side.

Those guys who were fortunate to live in Bridgeport and whose folks had connections with Old Man Daley and the 11th Ward Democratic Committee got the real gravy jobs. Charlie Rotkis had a great one: issuing tickets to blacks living in the Federal Street Public housing projects on 35th Street who were keeping unlicensed dogs. Fun then, but it would have a life expectancy nowadays of less than a Marine Corps officer in Korea! Other DeLaSalle buddies with connections wound up in cushy downtown City Hall do-nothing (but sell tickets to the mayor's fundraisers) jobs that any self-respecting guy would never do.

In a pinch of desperation we would sometimes head for West Madison Street and Skid Row and work for ReadyMen. Now that was an experience, working shoulder to shoulder with alkies and junkies of all types. Ex-doctors, ex-lawyers, ex-priests, ex-German paratroopers, everybody but us was an "ex" something. It was an education on the streets that you could not buy any other way. "Anybody ever work in lumber? Anybody here ever work in steel? OK, You, you, and you…get to work!" We got into the moving business in a big way too. We liked anything that was on the rough side with a strong physical bent so we could get into or stay in shape for football or baseball or whatever we were playing at the time.

Later on in the late '50s and after the military we hooked on to the Lake Carriers Association at 92nd and Commercial in South Chicago as temporary help on the ore boats. We were sent all over: up to Duluth and Two Harbors, Minnesota, out on the St. Mary's River and Detroit City. Even up to the Labrador through the Saint Lawrence Seaway. I usually served as a coal passer. Normally it was tolerable enough and the food was outstanding. The problem was when the automatic stokers broke down. Then we went on the "black-gang" mode: two hours on and four off. Temperatures would reach 120 degrees—a great way to get in shape for football. After a few shifts of hand feeding those insatiable fires and pulling red-hot clinkers, we would get totally disoriented. We were working under a maze of catwalks and could only see the outside light through a small door about three stories over our heads. If anything had gone wrong we would have been trapped down there like rats in a barrel. I still have a real sense of empathy for those poor guys on the Edmund Fitzgerald.

Also, we worked for Orv Sherman at Mayflower and Marvin Amstadter from Amstadter Movers over on Cottage Grove. The crazy thing was that Murph and I went into our own moving business: Pacific Movers. It was a great idea but real low overhead—we didn't have any. When a call came in we would estimate the job, bid it, and if successful go out and rent a truck based on the size of the job at hand. We had a great motto but little else: "For a Peaceful Move… Call Pacific!"

So we worked and hustled and eventually grew up. We became adults either the easy way or the hard way but we all did OK. We became teachers and school administrators, sales people, stock brokers, business-men, priests, brothers, or nuns, policemen, firemen, airline pilots —a host of jobs to support our families for many years and into retirement and the Great Hereafter.

"The finest teenager I ever knew was Slats Grobnik, who devoted his formative years to useless activities....He knew that in a few short years he would have to go out and get a job and begin doing something useful, and, on his 40th birthday, he did. As Slats always said about work: "if it's so good, how come they have to pay you to do it?"

- Mike Royko

23

KISSING THE "OLD DUMP" GOODBYE

In the late winter (or early spring) of 1999 as I was watching WGN, I saw a news story on our OLP: the "Old Ladies' Penitentiary" at 79th and Jeffery. Our Lady of Peace parish and school, in the infinite wisdom of the Archdiocese of Chicago, will be closing the school at the end of this school year. It would not see the millennium.

I felt a need to go back for one last nostalgic walk-through, so I called PJ, Phil Jordan, who was always ready to go back to the old neighborhood and we met at the school office on the 30th of March,1999. It was a shock to be back in the old school after five decades. I think I avoided it for so long because I wanted to remember the school and neighborhood the way it had been. I didn't know what to expect, but wasn't quite prepared for the wreckage and shabbiness, the air of benign and not-so-benign neglect: the sliding steel grates over the local store windows and vacant lots looking like bad dental work everywhere.

There was no graffiti anywhere on the church or the school, which I took to be a measure of respect from the local gangs for the mission of the parish and the services that it provides for the entire neighborhood. I parked right on 79th Street in front of the church, not realizing they had turned our old playground in back into a parking lot, probably because it is more secure.

The great church doors that had seen the Irish Catholics and now the Black Catholics come and go since 1933 were painted a plain terra-cotta. That change was as great a symbolic difference as I could imagine.

The old doors were a U.S. Mint dollar bill green. Rumor was that there were even colored threads like those in our currency either embedded in the paint itself or painted on in some faux art manner. I think I saw that when I was a kid. Or maybe I just started the rumor.

In any event, other than the hand-painted sign above the door (OUR LADY OF PEACE CHURCH) the exterior seemed little changed. The great Romanesque structure with the great bell tower, the black wrought-iron fence, the grim and stone-sober nuns' convent where we all stood outside one afternoon after school and demanded the return of one of our classmates from the aftermath of a schoolyard fight: "We want Willie! We want Willie!" Well, eventually we got Willie, but not before his mother showed up red-faced and ready to give him even more what-for than the good sisters already had.

I rang the bell at the rectory and could not help but take a look around at the corner of 79th and Jeffery. It was there in a way but in another way it was as gone as if it had never existed. Pla-Mor Lanes and the Tastee Freeze were obliterated. The Moline's great hamburger joint was now Herbert's Barber Shop. It would never again know one of the world's great culinary delights: the 15 cent greasy Mo-burger lathered in fried onions. I looked in vain for my old buddies lagging pennies in front of Mo's but they were all gone.

The rectory door opened and I was greeted by a pleasant young African-American man who had been prepped for my arrival. I had never been in the rectory before. The story in my family had been that my mother and father were married in this rectory. Not by choice but mandated by the powers that be because my dad was not Catholic. He did convert later and became a sword carrying, beplumed, and full fledged Knight of Columbus. Later on he would change back to his Anglicanism and then finally to Methodism in Conway, South Carolina where he lived until his death in 2000.

I was struck by how outmoded and outdated and small everything had become. Peeling dark brown paint on the wainscoted walls. Black and white bathroom tiles on the stair treads, dirty, gray terrazzo floors in the johns along with urinals tall enough for even a not-so-small boy to fall or get pushed into, fifteen foot classroom ceilings, thirteen foot glass windows, the square concrete columns in the basement where the "downstairs" church and kindergarten used to be.

A Head Start program is on the Chappel side now (some Jeffery wise guys would say that the Chappel side was always a kind of Head Start program), and there was a medical office for that day's asthma screening. The cloakrooms in every class gave us a clear feeling of a long time gone by. The school would need major rebuilding to be anywhere near functional today.

I had a strange flashback while waiting in the office for the current principal, Sister Lois Matusiak, OSF. When we were sent to the office it was not usually for a reward, although it was usually a just visit. When we left The Old Dump, as Studs Lonigan called his St. Ann's a little farther north, Sister DePorres was the principal. She was a definite no-nonsense kind of administrator, with an uncanny sense of what made us tick and what real children were all about. I don't know Sister Lois's educational philosophy, but she could not have been more gracious to PJ and me.

I had a sense of déjà vu and I realized that I had the same feeling when I went to the last White Sox home game at old Comiskey Park. It is time to let it go. It is finished! Go in peace because the Mass is ended! An era has ended. We went into the church for the first time in decades.

"OUR LADY OF PEACE – PRAY FOR US"

- Inscription over the main altar at OLP

Sister Lois was kind enough to take us into the old sacristy with at least a vestige of Latin on a yellowing card glued to the wooden cabinets. We went through the sacristy and out onto the main altar of the big Church: the holy of holies, the holy grail for at least two generations of Irish Americans from old South Shore.

SANCTUS; SANCTUS; SANCTUS.

The sacred words were still engraved into the altar steps behind the four tall polished wood pillars with the statues on top of Matthew, Mark, Luke and John. As altar boys we had been near petrified at the time of the consecration. It was not only the solemnity of the moment, but the sure and certain feeling of damnation if we made one mistake on that altar. Woe betide the boy that missed the consecration bells, mumbled his

Latin, or worse, forgot his place or fell asleep! Sister Estelle would be on his case like a shot!

We were glad to see that the old church has held up very well. The four tall columns with the evangelists are still imposing and the whole aura is that of genteel poverty, but certainly not neglect. You can see that this congregation is small but so far determined to keep the old place going. Amazingly, an order has finally been placed for a set of bells for the tower. A bright colored thermometer up by the main altar proclaims that the two year fund raising goal is $150,000. Old Father Rice must be looking on from somewhere and saying, "Right on, brothers!"

I appreciated all the time Sister Lois gave to take us through the church, the school and the basement. I appreciated the fact that she was from the south side. She was one of us and we had friends in common. After the tour, I asked Sister if we could go up into the tower for old time's sake but she very wisely begged off on that one. After she left us on our own for a while when PJ went over to St. Bride's to get his mother's baptismal certificate, I had an awful urge to go back to the tower entrance and sneak up one more time.

My rite of passage days must be over because I chickened out. I wish I could say that I tried the old trap door and it was locked, but I can't. Maybe I can redeem myself when we go back for the all-school reunion and walk-through for old grads the weekend after Memorial Day.

Memorial week will be an appropriate time to go back to the old dump. From its inception with Father Rice's return from WWI in 1919, to the Dominican sisters coming in 1923 to found the school, to the first graduating class in 1925, to my mom's class in 1928, to our graduation in 1952, through the Dominicans' departure back to Kentucky in 1973, to the changing of the neighborhood and the creation of a "full-service" school: a Head Start program with a medical and health center, this school means a lot to the area and the people of the neighborhood.

Regardless of whether you were of Irish descent and your family had worked on the I&M canal or you were descended from slaves and came from Vicksburg, Mississippi, if you went to OLP you had some strong feelings, mostly positive, about a special place and time in your life.

It was good to see the class pictures in the downstairs hallway. The first classes in the mid-twenties: boys in dark suits with parts down their middle, girls in light formal dresses, curls and all. The later classes with Afros but still dressed classier than ever. It was a shock to see my mother's bright but serious face peering out at me from the class of 1928. Then there we were in 1952. Caps and gowns on now, at the altar like some kind of group sacrifice while oblivious of the war in Korea and without a hint of the many profound social changes that were on their way.

The kindergarten pictures were also on display. They were down in the basement because that is where Sister Mary Louise held sway for over thirty years. Say what you want about the Dominican discipline, and there were few of us who did not feel the rap of their long, black rosary beads in a moment of errant behavior, but no one that I know has ever had a bad word to say about Sister Mary Louise Helmann from Nebraska.

Todays' children were getting ready for their school pictures. They were in Sunday best and proud as little peacocks. I took an opportunity to talk to a group of second and third graders and show them my notebook with our class pictures, some more than a half century old now. They seemed delighted and were as enthusiastic, bright, cheerful and as warm and accepting as they could possibly be. I have occasion to visit schools today in Wisconsin and am always struck by how casual many of the children are even asking sometimes, in an almost insolent way, "Who are you?" I cannot deny that is a very logical question to put to a visitor, but I cannot imagine us at OLP in the 1940s being that forward to an adult stranger.

This current generation of bright, absolutely delightful children is heartwarming. They laughed in amazement at our old school uniforms (girls only of course). They wanted to know, "Which one is your girlfriend?" I pointed to my little lost Kathleen Fitzgibbons and they all howled with cheerful laughter. We had our picture taken with these marvelously optimistic and energetic children. We wished them well in their journey. Some will go to St. Phillip Neri, St. Bride's over by the lake, St. Felicitas, St. Laurence, and St. Ailbe's over south on Stony Island.

Most though will wind up at Horace Mann Public School two blocks south on Chappel. I did mention to Dr. Sloan Letman, the current Pastoral Coordinator, whatever that is, the possibility of becoming a charter school. He indicated slyly with a wink and a nod, "We're working on that." Maybe there is a chance after all. I hope so.

The South Shore neighborhood has changed in many ways but I suspect the children are still similar. I wish that I would have thought to ask some of the boys: "Have you climbed up to the tower? Have you made that unique OLP rite of passage?" I did ask about line ball, "Ledge" and "Slaughteration" to see if some of the old playground games might have been passed down from class to class. They did not have a clue. At OLP these days basketball is king and you'd better believe it! Chicago Bulls posters are in evidence along with a championship plaque denoting that OLP had won the 1997 Catholic Youth Organization flag football sectional. It is a different generation altogether! That's alright. It should be! God bless!

24

MEMENTO MORI: OLP ALUMNI MASS

- Memorial Day, 1999

The cars and the white folks started coming into the old OLP playground early. Mass was not until 11:30 but you could see that this really was a special kind of day. A perfect day for an alumni mass and get-together: Memorial Day. A great day to remember our past and our families and those who put this grand magnificent structure together. It took a host of cakewalks, carnivals, donations, "New World" subscriptions and just plain hard work by many folks to put this whole place together and nourish it over the years. It was a bittersweet day for most of the "pink people" as Marie, my Italian-American sister-in-law calls the South Side Irish.

On the one hand was the incredible flood of memories: events, schoolyard games, battles, victories and defeats. People long gone now: grandparents, uncles,

cles, aunts, mothers, fathers, brothers and sisters. Our people are either in cemeteries all over the area or else moved on to the southern and western suburbs: Homewood, Flossmoor, Mokena, Hinsdale, Western Springs.

That seemed to be an unwritten rule. If you left the old neighborhood, you never went north; at least not to the North side. You somehow stayed connected to the neighborhood by staying in line with it. Maybe we just wanted to be ready in case it all came back again someday, resurrected in all its Irish-American glory with the Knights of Columbus ready to do battle with their Admiral of the Ocean Sea feather hats and their filigreed Wilkinson swords. Up at O'Halloran's tavern on 79th you had to check your sword behind the bar after K of C get-togethers in case someone got carried away with a bit too much of the sauce and too much of the temper.

The important thing was then, is now, and shall ever be, the people. Like my cousin, Dr. Bruce Hannon from the University of Illinois once said: "Good people make a good place good!" It was wonderful to see at least some of the class of '52: Jim Sherman, 'Mac' Corley, Maureen Kaveny, Terry Ann Turner, Brother David Adelsbach, Peggy Delaney, Pat (aka Sister Jean) Hughes, Phil Jordan, Josie Wall and yours truly. Attendees from other classes just before us or soon after were Leo (Kickapoo Inn) DelGrasso, Jim Boushelle, Hank Grannon, Terry Dunn, Bernie Judge, John Coppe, and Eddie Lyons, just to name a few. Where were the missing ones though? Bo, Tom McCue, the Murph, Harry Gerrity, Mick, John and Renee (Burnjas) Hart? Where were Jack Sheehan, Bob Smith, Dick Bringaze, the Melaniphys, Artie Larson, Kathleen Fitzgibbons, Judy Coyle, Barbara Powell, Elise Bundesen and Eileen Gavigan? JoAnn Rinella, where were you? Van Snyder, where have you gone? Are you still playing ball for No-

Notre Dame, Dick Prendergast? Bill Drew and Timmy McNamara (our grade school coaches), why weren't you there when the roll was called? Howie Reed: are you still coaching somewhere? It was always easier to keep track of the guys because they did not change their names—aliases maybe, but not names. I must admit though that the Acquinas alums do keep in touch with each other as well or better than the guys seem to have done.

The church itself was in good shape and the mass, though long, went well. There were over 500 "pink people" in attendance. I got the feeling that I was seeing that wonderful film, Cinema Paradiso, again when the villagers assemble for the last time to see the demolition of their old theater. Some of the faces were so familiar but I couldn't place them until they introduced themselves or someone else told me who they were.

The milling and greetings went past 11:30 until I thought Father (technically Monsignor, but always 'Father Mac' to us) McDermott was going to get up on the great altar and start chastising us: "This isn't some kind of flop house! Get together you people, this is the Lord's House and we need some respect here. If you want to party, why don't you just take a hike around the block..."

Luckily for us, Father Mac has calmed down these days and has mellowed out as well. It was a beautiful mass. Our Lady of Peace does not even have a full time priest anymore, if you can believe that. It is technically a "mission" church now. A lovely old parishioner told me later over punch and cookies that when they recently requested a priest from the Archdiocese, they were told, "If you find one, you can have him!"

I am going to write to our own Father Bill Maher and Father Terry Figel and let them know that here is a fine opportunity to finish up their great and long careers in a most wonderful way. Why not? Certainly stranger things have happened in this church and in other places.

The choir and the organist were small in number, but superb singers and musicians. We certainly never saw or heard the like when we were growing up. These folks had soul. They simply sang our butts off, to be honest. They were truly great and even the somewhat stiff and formal audience warmed up to them and gave them a round of applause from time to time. My daughter jabbed me in the ribs, however, when I asked her if she'd like to see me do some back flips down the main aisle a la "The Blues Brothers".

The only religious people missing were our old nuns. The five survivors from our era are all down at St. Catherine's in Kentucky near Bardstown and the home of Jim Beam, Jack Daniels and American Bourbon whisky. Our old principal, Sister DePorres, is still living in the Motherhouse along with Sister Vallina. Sister Mary Louise, our kindergarten teacher, is in the infirmary with Sister Estelle, who supervised both the patrol boys and the altar boys. Sister Genevieve, who specialized in teaching music, is also in the infirmary but is doing quite nicely under circumstances in her purple jogging suit (was nothing sacred after Vatican II?)

Communion was a more than special time, bringing back a flood of memories of a long line family and friends who went to that same marble rail over the decades with the same feelings of hope and circumstance. My favorite memory will always be that my wife and daughter and I were able to come together with that whole lost line of family and friends again. The crowning glory however, was getting a kiss from Sister Jean (Pat Hughes) as she was coming back from communion. I had waited 50 years for that!

After mass we wandered on our own through the entire school. Most folks headed for the tables which were loaded with goodies people brought along, served with punch and coffee by some wonderful parishioners who could not have been more open and welcoming.

People could not get enough of the "rogue's gallery" of graduates on the first floor or the kindergarten pictures in the basement. We met Mr. Samuel Morris, custodian extraordinaire. He is a true and dapper gentleman and a scholar in the E.A. Griffin mold. He told us some great stories and let it be known that he still has a key to the tower. Phil and I now have a deal with him. He will let us up the old tower for a last look around this summer sometime. We are going to take him up on that and bring along a fifth of Jack Daniels. Maybe we'll all three of us just go up to the second level and have a memorable afternoon!

ITE, MISSA EST

The mass has ended. Things will go on. Sister Lois is on her way to St. Isidore's in Blue Island now and we are back on our respective life journeys.

Maybe we are like salmon. Maybe we have been imprinted early on with a need to go back home regardless of the journey we are on. I hope that we all can learn from this experience and that we will carry it on in some way. Even if we are in the 'burbs, or downtown, or Michigan, Wisconsin, Colorado, California, or Florida, we will always be a part of this old parish and we can still be connected. I hope that the Alumni Mass becomes a new annual tradition for all of us: a time of reconciliation, renewal and healing.

I hope that we can pick up what Sister Lois and Dr. Letman have begun and carry it to a new level. Why can't we create an OLP Alumni Association that can preserve the past and also make a real and lasting contribution to the present parishioners?

25

A MOTHER'S DAY POEM

Our Lady of Peace:
A Mother's Day Poem for
Our Sisters of Saint Catharine of Siena

A long way from St. Catharine's down in Kentucky.
Chicago: "Urbs in Horto" they called it.

SOUTH SHORE DAYS – 1940's & '50's

Latin for "City in a Garden."
A City in a Garden called South Shore.
You created a garden for us: a Victory Garden.
Ruly and unruly we were in the morning of our youth.

Sister Mary Louise. (Kindergarten)
You took our mothers' places and you gave us room to grow.
You could fly. I remember it well.
We would go out over on the Jeffery
side of the playground and you would soar.
Up, over and around the bell-less bell tower.
"Come up! Come up!" you cried. We loved it.
We weren't ready yet.
Later on though, we did fly.
We climbed that tower and others. Unafraid.

Sister Catharine Joseph. (First grade)
Serious you were. We weren't.
We probably gave each other mutual fits.
You are in "La Sata" now, "Place of Peace."
Well, we had our moments.
Rest in peace.

Sister Margaret Ann. (Second grade)
Our Irish came out on the playground,
Along with the things we carried:
tops and balls, bottle caps, spare change,
Duncan yo-yos, knives, string and chalk, notes.
We were collectors. Still are.
Memories now.
Good ones.
Peace.

Sister Villana. (Third grade)

A MOTHER'S DAY POEM

A Southern lady.
You supported us and watched over us
when you took our mothers' places.
An icon in black and white; gentle, giving.
In all of you we saw our mothers' faces.
At least we do now.

Sister Anna. (Fourth grade)
The world was on fire but curiously
all we knew was peace from you-
Peace in our urban garden.
The old church was born in 1919.
The first sisters came in 1923.
"Our Lady of Peace" they called her:
"We've had enough of war," said young Father Rice.
(You remember reading about it: "the war to end wars.")
That's a good one! Thanks for the thought.
Our time will come later.

Sister Lorenz. (Fifth grade)
"More cannon fodder" said the nurse as she brought my
brother Donnie out to meet my mother in 1942
Sad thing to say on such a joyous occasion.
Sorrows are in the future.
While now is now.
Pray for peace.
Prepare for war!

Sister Innocent. (Sixth grade)
We called you Sister "Guilty."
We didn't mean it though. (South side Irish humor is
all.)
You protected us and sheltered us and nurtured us: Giv-
ing.
Cracked down at first, then you lightened up.

PJ bolts class suddenly: Lightning temper in a bottle!
Soon he came back.
We all did.
Peace.

Sister Ann. (Seventh grade)
The best of times and the worst of times.
Mr. Dickens was right.
Complex, emotional.
Hard to figure. Loved your "cakewalks" though.
You meant well. You and Mr. Warp.
Kearney, Nebraska.
We wish you peace.

Sister Lucille. (Eighth grade)
Ah, "Lulu" you were so gently miscast.
I wish you were here. I'd apologize.
Didn't mean to argue the whole year
about the flat earth theory.
It was fun though.
Had a good argument going until

A MOTHER'S DAY POEM

I saw the shots from NASA.
You were right.
We are living on a fragile blue sphere.
It is round.
A fragile garden-globe.
"Horto in space"
Pax Vobiscum.

Sister DePorres our Principal
Administration is never easy.
Can't please everyone, you know!
You were fair.
We got whacked from time to time.
Usually had it coming.
If we didn't, well, it prepared us for life.
Gave us resiliency.
"Got a lot worse at home," we'd say.
Good to tell stories now.
Like two Depressionaires comparing their poverty:
"I really got it that time for the fight on the playground!
You should have seen the other guy!"

Warm, flybuzzed, drowsy, sweet Chicago spring days.
Windows open.
Green boughed and sweet-scented.
Flowered altars graced the rooms.
Mary reigns supreme.
Peace be with you.
Freedom is not far away now.
Baseball, lagoons, beaches. The lake.
Summer peace.
Heat.
Dona Nobis Pacem.
Give us peace.
Thank you for everything.

26

MISSION ACCOMPLISHED!

- Boxing Day 1996, St. Catharine's, Kentucky

Phil Jordan, PJ and I left old Bardstown for home on December 28, 1996 with the sun shining bright on our "Old Kentucky Home," the Motherhouse of the Dominican Sisters of St. Catharine. The weather on this farewell morning was gloriously spring-like: 65 degrees, green grass, birds everywhere, and sunlight breaking out between the white rollers overhead.

We had done what we wanted to do despite Wisconsin and Michigan blizzards and thousands of holiday drivers. We had made a trip of rediscovery, reconciliation and thanksgiving to see our old nuns, our first teachers from our youth. We had a lot to think about. We had a lot to digest.

It had been exactly a half century since we were in third grade at Our Lady of Peace with Sister Vallina. Our own Sister "Vanilla". We, and they, had covered some ground since then. Our gifted classmate, Terry

Tobin, had visited some time ago and described the place as "a massive red brick Victorian pile." It was an apt description that we could not miss as we came around a sweeping curve on the Bardstown Road between Bardstown and Springfield in the "Holy Land" of Northern Kentucky.

The reminders were all around us on our map: towns of Nazareth, Solitude, and Trappist, (with the brooding Gesthemeni Abbey of Thomas Merton), St. Mary's, Calvary, Mt. Pisgah, St. Francis and lastly, our goal: St. Catharine's—our own OLP Motherhouse! We might be in the Bible Belt, but at least it was our own bible! We stood before the old, flaky white-lettered sign above the main entrance, which read simply:

St. Catharine's
1904

Perhaps it was the fog and "gloomarainy" mist, but there was a distinctly Dickensian air about the place, a kind of Dotheby Girls Hall genteel seedy look to the place. One bolt of lightning and PJ and I would have been out of there in a flash! Though set in a land of beauty, there was no welcome sign and you could not help but feel the somber and apprehensive mood of those young girls of long ago who had walked up those now worn steps.

Young Mary Louise Helman walked up these stairs from Hastings Nebraska, so did Catherine Joseph, and Margaret Ann, and Vallina Sheeran from Louisville, and Innocent, and Lorenz, and Anna and Ann from Kearney, Nebraska and Lucille and DePorres, and Geneva and Estelle, and a host of others.

Who is left? Where are they all now? Will any of those who are left remember either of us? Was any of it all real? Was there really a Father Rice and did he actually build a church of peace in the South Shore neighborhood of Chicago in 1919? Was there really a portable church at one time at 79th and Jeffery? Was there a Monsignor named "His Royal Highness" Friel? Did he have a WWI shell-shocked brother named Joe? Where did they come from and where did they go?

Well, they came from Boston and the east, and a whole contingent came from Nebraska for some reason, and they came from Kentucky. Some to escape poverty, boredom and a grinding Depression, some offered up by their families, some with a zeal we don't see anymore. The population of the house is aged now. The youngest woman we met was the old housekeeper from down the road who buzzed around us during our entire visit.

It is truly a house of antiques like those shops we saw in Bardstown. Eighteen foot lace-curtained windows of glass held in by the original wood frames. I had the feeling that if something is not done soon, the house will become a massive pile of Victorian red-bricks.

We were on a mission. Phil said it was a mission from God like the Blues brothers, Jake and Elwood. I'm not sure, but it was an interesting trip. We flipped a coin to see who was going to ring the bell. Phil lost. Suddenly a grimfaced older woman appeared. She slid suddenly up to the door window, and caught us by surprise. The door opened a crack. We explained who we were. I mentioned Sister Ann Miriam Hickey. She did not smile but does let us in. I got a flashback to a call to the office at OLP years earlier, and felt the same way. We introduced ourselves, but she did not. I named her "Sister Suspicious." Sister Suspicious Aloysius, O.P. She grilled us: "What do you want? Where are you from? Whom do you want to see? Why?" What did we want indeed? What were we doing there? Why had we traveled such a great distance to reconnect with a past that is long gone? Isn't it better to let the past go and remember how it was in the bright days of our youth? Why look for the grim reality of today? Did we have any business there? The questions she raised were very real indeed. Yet somehow I felt that we had every right to be there and that the trip did have a real purpose—a mission perhaps of internal discovery and certainly of thanksgiving. Let someone else decide. I got the feeling that persistence would beat Sister Suspicious.

She asked for our business cards. Phil was prepared, and whipped his out. Luckily I found a dog-eared one that I had been sitting on. She collected them without a word and slid silently out of the room. We looked at each other. What were we doing here? Had this long journey been for nothing?

I talked to the housekeeper. I thought she might have been a postulant assigned housekeeping duties in a spirit of humility. She was a local. She was employed. There are no young ones who used to do all the menial tasks. There are just no young women at all. An ancient way of life is disappearing.

I was looking to see if I could sneak a souvenir out of the waiting room but Sister Suspicious suddenly slid back in. I was hoping she couldn't read minds. She informed us that my correspondent, Sister Ann Miriam Hickey, the archivist of the house, was in the infirmary. I was getting the impression that everyone was in the infirmary and that this whole place, like old Spalding Hall in Bardstown during the Civil War, had become a kind of military hospital for the religious.

She said crisply that, "Sister Ann does not wish to see anyone!" I seemed to hear a giant gate closing with a reverberating clang. I showed her our notebooks, our writings and asked about any of the nuns from OLP in the 1940s and 1950s. Phil rattled them off chronologically. We mentioned Father Mac. Anything to allay her suspicions.

We knew that our old kindergarten teacher, Sister Mary Louise, was in the Sansbury infirmary next to the main building. We must have mentioned Sister Vallina specifically. Sister Suspicious slid away. We never saw her again.

Miraculously, Sister Maria appeared. An angel of mercy, she smiled; she said she was familiar with Chicago and although she was not at OLP, she knew many of our nuns and she is very fond of Chicago, having served up on the North Side. She informed us that Sister Vallina was upstairs and asked if we wanted to visit with her. We had arrived. We were home!

We were seated in the waiting room when Sister Vallina was ushered in. We stood, smiled and greeted her. She was in fine fettle. Shocked. Really shocked. "No one," she said in wonder, "no one from the OLP days has ever come to visit!" She went on and on about little Jimmy O'Neill. Twerp was ahead of us, we guess. PhD in physics from Berkeley. Used to stay in touch with her for many years. Then he took a sabbatical leave, traveled off somewhere and the letters suddenly stopped. It took some doing to get her off the subject of the damn lost Jimmy O'Neill. Perhaps he'll show up on the internet someday. Maybe even stop by St. Catharine's. Goodbye Jimmy. Now get lost again! We've got some serious talking to do.

We shared our old report cards. I asked her if she would change some of my grades. Obedience and deportment were going down the drain fast. I got the feeling I was "socially promoted" to prevent her from having another year like that one. She did say that overall we were good kids. In her career she had more than 1000 students. How could anyone remember two from 50 years ago? She tried. We taped the interview and the thoughts went on.

We came to realize that our old Sister "Vanilla" was in reasonably good health, and thank God or George Burns, she was not in the infirmary. She was a delightful southern lady still. Her only drawback was that she was suffering from a severe case of "virtual verbosity". It was as though someone released suddenly from a vow of silence had been given a dispensation to tell everything from the past half century and had to get it all out before we disappear.

We heard about Monsignor Friel and his $10 Christmas gift to every nun (generous with our collections, wasn't he?) He also went up and down 79th Street every Saturday looking for the "best cuts of meat—for the Sisters, you know!" (I'll bet. I'm sure he and Nick the janitor got their cuts too).

Saturday mornings were a special treat. All the nuns from OLP and most of Chicago were guests at a movie theater owned by the St. Ignatius parish up on the Northwest side. "Going My Way" she said, "all the good ones..." Legion of Decency, I'm sure. Forget Jane Russell in The Outlaw. Saturday was also shopping day. Not that you can do a whole lot of shopping on $30 a month. The Fair Store had a special deal. Through a codicil in a will, all nuns were to be given a free cafeteria-style meal when shopping at the Fair Store. One problem: if they ate more than they should or took too many items over the prescribed nunly amount, they then got a surcharge. Wasn't that justice?

Suddenly, who slid in but our old principal, Sister DePorres (fondly known as "DePorridge") Then we were stunned! She was as cheerful and crusty as you could imagine. She was a long way from the infirmary and couldn't go out to lunch with us because she had other pressing appointments and was a lady on the go. She was as sharp as a tack and I got the feeling she could still take over a school and do a better job than most. She was, by her own admission, "happy, happy, happy!" Originally from Kearney, Nebraska, she knew Sister Ann and Sister Ann's family very well. We didn't push that issue too much about the toughest teacher we ever had.

I asked her about the tall tower and if she knew that we rascals were climbing up there with some regularity. She then said something interesting, thinking of the society of litigation we have become. She said she knew that we were going up there, but believed that "boys need to challenge things," needed a 'rite of passage' activity. She said that janitor Nick Rollins wanted the tower locked and sealed off but she said no and kept it technically off-limits, fully realizing that it would be a testing ground for generations of young boys. (Question: did any girls make the famous tower climb?)

She must have been on to something when you think how "Super Don" DeLaMar made a career of flying and skydiving. He and I were both in the 101st Airborne together. He later taught John Coppe as well as Johnny Mack to fly. Tom Murphy has had his own plane as has classmate Harry Gerrity in California. Father Terry Figel has made a career in the U.S. Air Force as a chaplain and has come back recently from a military flight round trip to Germany to visit his former parishes and parishioners in Denmark. Could Sister DePorres' philosophy have anything to do with all that interest in aviation?

She remembered the old days at OLP very fondly. She was there until 1957.

She recalled the infamous Gerrity-Bayuk schoolyard battle very well. In detail, even. That was incredible! Worth the trip itself! Better yet, upon taking our leave to go gallivanting, she stood up, shook her black adjustable aluminum cane at me and warned, "Young man, now you behave yourself—this is Holy Ground you know!" I know! (Why would she pick on me? I was being as good as I could be.) Then she slid out to her luncheon.

Sister Geneva decided she was not up to going out to lunch with us at the last minute, so we buckled Sister "Vanilla" in and took her back to Bardstown for lunch. Can you imagine that? What a day! Back up the winding Bardstown road with its beautiful views. I want to go back around Easter time. Spring can be glorious in those parts!

Bardstown was a real delight, a kind of Middle-Southern Williamsburg, filled with antique shops, religious stores, restaurants, a state park, a movable dining train, its own cathedral (St. Joseph's) and a host of art galleries, book stores and gift shops galore. The Lincolns stayed at the Talbot tavern downtown after losing their Kentucky homestead in a lawsuit and while on the way to Indiana, and eventually to Illinois, where the rest would be history.

Speaking of history, Bardstown really got hit during the Vietnam War. An Army National Guard unit from Bardstown was mauled in one battle and lost 16 young men killed in that engagement. This from a little town which only has a population of 7,500 today. There is a memorial to those soldiers up at the courthouse in the middle of the town square and you can imagine what the funerals were like. In November of '96, you may remember Bardstown in the national news. The Jack Daniels whiskey distillery caught fire and did millions of dollars worth of damage. Thank God, no lives were lost, but have you ever seen grown men cry?

We stopped first at Xavier's Restaurant in Old Spalding Hall—the former Seminary and Civil War military hospital. We had met the owner, Bill Ellis, the night before while looking to get some supper. Something about the place, and I must admit it was confusing, turned Sister off and she asked if we could go to Dagwood's on Main Street. So off we went. We got settled in to what she thought was Dagwood's when we found out that Dagwood's was up one more block. So, off we went again, cane and all. This time it was the right place. At first I thought that anyone who doesn't get out very much would be happy to get anything. Just the opposite seems to be true. When you think about it, she was right: the less you get out, the more you want to make sure you get to the right place!

We had a great lunch, with Sister getting her Southern-style catfish. We done good! She even told the waitress, who nodded politely as waitresses will, about "her boys" whom she had taught so many years ago in Chicago, who had come to see her after all these many years.

She gave us the grand tour back at St. Catharine's. The old chapel has been remodeled. The centerpiece rose window up behind the altar is just magnificent and is a real must see. There is a two-year junior college on the grounds, called St. Catharine's, of course. She took us to the Priory Church of St. Rose, which is just across the hills and within sight of St. Catharine's, not five minutes away. It has beautiful high grounds with a gorgeous view and is in a lovely old part of Kentucky. The church was open. It was a dead ringer for small country churches that you see all up and down England. Norman style with a small bell tower and lichens all over the old stone exterior walls. Statues and eyes everywhere and on the front altar a double crucifix (figure front and back), something I had not seen before. I suspect that the Romans didn't think of it, or they would have used it just to save wood. We went back to St. Catharine's, where we went to the Sansbury infirmary and met for a visit with Sister Mary Louise, our former kindergarten teacher and Sister Geneva our music teacher. Not having any musical talent, I don't remember Sister Geneva as much, but do remember Sister Mary Louise very well.

Our kindergarten year was 1943-44, to put things in perspective. Sr. Mary Louise was dressed in white from head to foot. Her hair was white as snow. She was thoughtful, thin, frail, almost transparent. She was wracked and crippled with rheumatoid arthritis and unable to get out at all anymore. Her mind was just as sharp as ever and she recalled those kindergarten days very well. It was something of a miracle that our nuns could have dealt with classes the size they were. Maybe we were not as bad as we thought we were.

She said she was strict but I don't recall that at all. Get Phil to tell you about the time he couldn't get out of his snowsuit. I think he rolled around the hallway for a whole half day until the bell rang. Then he was in good shape because he was all ready to go. Good thing he didn't have to go the bathroom. Reality is when you've got a big class you can't leave them to go get some kid out of his snowsuit.

We had a long talk. Sister "Vanilla" kept things going whenever there was a lull. Out in the hallway, we met Sister Estelle. She was on the Jeffery side and in charge of the altar boys and the patrol boys, as I recall. She as a lot smaller than I remembered her, but then we were a little bigger now too. Her sister, who is also a nun, works with Father Ignatius McDermott at Haymarket House on West Washington Street in Chicago.

It was a bittersweet goodbye but we assured them that they were not forgotten and that they were loved and remembered fondly by everyone we were still in contact with. We promised to come back.

We turned and headed south for the Abbey of Our Lady of Gethsemani, the one-time home of Thomas Merton, author of The Seven Storey Mountain. It was getting dark and we had miles to go before we could sleep - but we were headed home again.

27

TRANSUBSTANTIATION

- A minor miracle at St. Catharine's, Kentucky

The old nun was as serious as could be. You could tell she was serious - serious as she was right after recess fifty years ago when she would try to get us back on track for religion class after we had had twenty glorious minutes of "Slaughteration" under our belt. "Mischievous," she called us now. That was a kind way to put it. We thought we were a grand group of hell raisers. I suppose every class that came through Our Lady of Peace school during the entire half century the Kentucky Dominicans were at OLP, from 1923 to 1973, thought they were the wildest and toughest group of kids to ever roam the old playground behind the school between Chappel Avenue and Jeffery Boulevard.

"I'll never forget it," she said wistfully, her eyes dimmed with age, but not her memory. "We had this old television here at the house." You could tell how she put it in her southern drawl that that TV was mighty important. Mighty important indeed. It was the good Sisters' only real link to the outside world. Walter Cronkite, Bishop Fulton J. Sheen, Dave Garraway, and Ed Sullivan on Sunday nights in the big old red brick Victorian pile of a manse that sprawled across the shining brow above the Bardstown Road.

"It was the nicest set, but I think we held on to it a little too long." "Sometimes," she murmured, "I think we hold on to too many things too long around here."

We weren't sure exactly whether she was talking to herself or to us. The reverie continued: "We loved that old TV but of course we had rules about what we could see and how long we could watch things in the evening before our night prayers."

"Yes, indeed, we sure did watch that TV. That was in the old days of course, before every religious group split up into little communities!"

"Lordy, if we split up into any more communities, we won't have any community at all. We'll just have as many communities as we have sisters in the house. Won't that be a fine kettle of catfish! Why have any community at all then?"

On and on she went. The years were passing backwards like in one of those old 1940s movies with the calendar dates flying off all over the screen like autumn leaves when a car speeds down an October street in Chicago and you could still burn leaves in the gutters.

"The TV was a Zenith. Best model they made," she stated proudly. Where it had come from and exactly how long ago, no one in the house could say except perhaps for Mother Superior. This was obviously before they had a position in the house called a "coordinator."

These details and the nitty-gritty nuances related to guarantees and warranties were left to the coordinator. She would have known, but of course they didn't have coordinators back then.

"After so many years," here she sighed a bit, "the TV finally began to go. It developed a kind of ghost and that ghost really messed up that picture."

"We prayed and prayed but it didn't help, at least not directly at the time." You could tell that not only was the TV one very powerful influence in the limited lives of our old sisters, but also that something momentous was about to happen.

Somehow they got the TV repair man to come out all the way from Louisville. He must've been a Protestant because he gave them a quote of $250 to repair the set.

"Why even then we wouldn't have known whether it would have stayed fixed," she stated knowingly. "We just knew that we didn't have that kind of money. We just prayed," she said softly. "We just watched and prayed like the apostles in the upstairs room after the resurrection."

"Then one day, while I was in the room, the big sitting room where we always had the old TV, I don't think that it was even on, I was all by myself really. I heard a 'pop' sound inside the set and the TV just cranked up by itself. Something happened inside that set. When I turned it on, it had the finest picture we'd ever seen!"

You could tell that she thought it miraculous. Maybe not a first class, world class kind of miracle like Charlton Heston's parting of the Red Sea, or the 1969 New York Mets, or the miracle of the loaves and fishes, but it was one important minor league miracle.

I was surprised and didn't know exactly how to deal with all this so I just said nothing and Phil did the same. I don't think we even talked about the incident to ourselves. What do you really say in the face of such overwhelming blind faith?

Someone, ironically on TV recently, said that "Saints and cynics are very similar and very close to each other. They both see the world quite clearly in many of the same ways. The great, and maybe the only, difference is faith. The saint believes on faith alone, and the cynic doubts on faith alone."

You know this is a cynical age. Yet it was really something to see our old teacher and her unwavering faith in this miracle: the miracle of the Zenith at St. Catharine's.

You know the miracle of the young: we were celebrating the miracle of the old in the house of antiques near Bardstown in Kentucky at Christmas. The visitation of the two wise guys from the north: G.J. and P.J.

I began to think about the many miraculous things that we take for granted in our modern lives. It was a miracle that we were even down here in the Motherhouse of our old nuns from OLP. It was miraculous that all of us OLPers are still in contact after all these years.

Our families are a minor miracle to us. It was a miracle that as many of us survived Chicago, let alone got to the age we now find ourselves.

Miraculous that we could have found our way in education and the training that we have been blessed with. A miracle that we could have had as much peace in our lifetime as we had: missing one world war, a police action, and Vietnam as well as the Gulf conflict, Iraq, Afghanistan and a host of brushfire wars.

I think the point is it all depends on how you look at the world. If you see a self-healing TV as a miracle, then you are bound to see the world through miraculous eyes. Everything to that kind of person becomes an exercise in faith. I still look at our office copy machine that way. It's very evident to me that there is simply an almost infinite number of atom-sized Dominican monks inside, whirling away at incredibly high speeds to make copies for us.

Is that a miracle or what? If our world-view is everything, then how wonderful it must be to see everything around us as miraculous. Even the self-repairing Zenith TV. Maybe that is the real message of transubstantiation. We live in a world of miracles where anything can happen - and usually does.

28

EPILOGUE: LIFE STORIES: FACT AND/OR FICTION

I began wondering why the stories about the old South Shore neighborhood and our youth are so intriguing to me. Why are they important? What is their value and their significance? Why do most of us like them? Why do some of us avoid them and try to block them out?

What can we gain from our collective experiences? From what Lincoln called, "The Mystic Chords of Memory" How can we preserve this common culture that we share - who can we give it to and can other generations appreciate these stories?

While contemplating these and other mysteries of the universe, I came across a couple of articles that helped me put this into a new perspective. The first is an article by Frank H. Wood that I received in a professional journal for those working with students with severe emotional and behavioral problems.

EPILOGUE: LIFE STORIES

The other material is from the introduction of a new book of Clarence Darrow's own writings in which he is talking about an earlier autobiographical work he called "Farmington." In "Farmington" Darrow seems to be going through many of the feelings that we are going through right now. First the lesson:

"Behavior is determined by a person's mental representation of reality. Such representations consist of a person's subjective interpretations of events, emotions, actions, people, and other aspects of his or her world, and of the causal, motivational, and enabling relations between them. They reflect a person's understanding of past events, direct the interpretation of future experiences and, more importantly, guide behavior."

- Van den Broek and Thurlow (1991)

"As individuals, we are intensely interested in our life stories and those of others. A vast library of print and other media material has been developed in response to this interest. Besides the memoirs and biographies in which purportedly true individual life stories are made public, fictional accounts are very popular. Many consumers of these stories probably have difficulty maintaining the boundary between fact and fantasy, if indeed fact is fact and fantasy is fantasy."

- Frank H. Wood

This is me. I never let a good story get too bogged down by too much truth. On the other hand, some of the true things that have happened to me are "stranger than fiction." Here is one last example.

How could anyone logically explain meeting an old black gentleman on the South Side of Chicago, lean and straight as an arrow, and dressed in a Civil War Union general's dress uniform. He was immaculate, tall and proud in every sense, right down to his red sash and dress sword.

He, myself, my wife and two daughters, meet at Stephen Douglas' tomb on 35th Street one warm Memorial day and he invites us to follow follow him home after the ceremonies (he and his wife are driving a mint green Cadillac with gold trim) to a most beautiful lannonstone funeral home complete with the artwork of mortuary practices around the world and a shining gold King Tut sarcophagus in the lobby.

Upon arrival, the first thing we notice (remember we are at 3232 South King Drive) is the "Stars and Bars" Confederate battle flag flying over the place. He has a museum dedicated to the memory of the thousands of Confederate prisoners of war who died at Camp Douglas and who are buried at Oakwoods Cemetery. The flag and the museum have gone over like a "lead balloon" in the 'hood, but he has kept the museum open and the flag flying under threats of harm on a regular basis.

Above the gorgeous funeral home, on the second floor, is a working Music Hall. The community hall and its memorabilia are devoted to the memory of his parents who once owned a music store on State Street in old 'Bronzeville'.

When he bought the property in the late '50's he did not realize that his grandfather had been trained in a black Illinois cavalry regiment on that very site. He has since devoted his life to telling the story to people, all people, about Camp Douglas and the sacrifice of the men on both sides who lived and died there.

EPILOGUE: LIFE STORIES

He is Mr. E.A. Griffin and one of his most momentous funerals was that for Jesse Owens at Rockefeller Chapel on the campus of the University of Chicago.

Was that fact or fantasy? How could I make this up? I don't know but I'm glad my wife and girls were there because they always accuse me of blending the thin line between fact and fantasy a little too much. Reminds me: Jack McDonnell and I once met Steppin Fetchit in the Pago-Pago lounge. We traded stories and drinks until the wee hours of the morning-but that's another story...

"Individual life stories incorporate elements of the group life stories shared with others. In Daniel Quinn's novel, "Ishmael," Ishmael defines culture as "a people enacting a (shared) story,... their group scenario interrelating man, the world, and the gods" (1995, p. 41).

"We can more easily understand the present behavior of others and assist them in developing socially acceptable, personally satisfying behavior as we become familiar with the blend of individual and group elements of their stories."

"Learning how others explain their past experiences to themselves, how they regard the present, and their anticipations of the future is an on-going, serial process. Life stories are developed over time - and may undergo changes in the telling and re-telling."

- Frank H. Wood

In 1904 Clarence Darrow, age 47, wrote "Farmington", a semi-autobiographical novel of his own childhood set in rural America, during the Civil War and post-war period. Darrow was from the little town of Kinsman,

Ohio on the Shenengo River Lake almost into Pennsylvania.

At the age of seventy-five, in a preface to the book's 1932 edition Darrow wrote:

"There is no purpose in this story, and no lesson can be gleaned from its reading. It is neither fact nor fiction. But still, I could take my readers to a little town in Ohio that is much like Farmington. I could show them the old swimming hole and the places where the fishes refused to bite.

I could point out the boys and girls who are still outside the graveyard fence, though the few who linger are headed in that direction, and are now quite near the gate that so often opened to let my neighbors in, but never by any chance swung wide enough to let them out.

I doubt if any of these old boys and girls will recognize the pictures I have drawn. Their eyes have grown dim, and their memories vague, and they may not recall how important life was then, for our childhood in Farmington lasted such a little while, and was so long ago."

"The years are flying fast, and I am going farther and farther from Farmington, but my wandering thoughts are ever returning to that land of dreams, recalling the faces that are no more, and the memories that remain.

I need not tell the reader that some of these sketches are real, or were 'once upon a time.' Nothing is strictly true in a world of constant change. Still, as one who is living beyond his time, I find that the images and recollections of my youth are more alluring than the people and scenes that greet me now. I am aware that this picture of the boys and girls and men and women that I knew is really a composite one, a blend of them all.

Even my own form and personality of other days eludes me, and I do not at all realize that I am looking at my face when I scan old photographs of myself, however hard I try to remember just how things seemed and how really I felt."

- Clarence Darrow, 1932

I enjoyed a review of a 1904 book by "The Dial" which I feel may apply to this story:

"It is a book for boys, for women - but above all, it is a book for men who have once been boys."

- The Dial, October 16th, 1904

Does this look backward make any more sense now? They say, "You can't go home again." Of course Thomas Wolfe was right. But in a very real sense you can go home again in your memories and shared remembrances. I guess the thing to do is not to lose sight of the future.

But I wouldn't trade any of today's kids one day for some of the times and the memories we have had in old South Shore.

LaVergne, TN USA
02 June 2010
184676LV00001BA/71/P

9 780578 024776